CONTENTS

Can You Build a Better Brain?

A lot of myths about the brain float through our culture. I don't know about you, but I grew up on many of them and assumed they were supported by hard facts. It was only when I came to study the actual science behind them (first in university classrooms as a student, later in the laboratory as a neurologist) that I realized that most of them are really just myths—and can actually prevent you from getting your brain into peak condition, maximizing your ability to think, learn, remember, and even enjoy life. Here's what I mean.

Myth #1: You only use 10 percent of your brain

Of the many myths, this is my favorite. Sometimes, it's said, geniuses like Einstein managed to use more than the 10 percent, so that's why they were so smart.

Fair enough—it's natural to think that the brain of a scientist such as Einstein, who was so good at using his brain, might be slightly different. And in fact, there is some evidence that this is the case. However, it's unlikely that Einstein used a higher percentage of his brain than you do, because in the brain—whether it's yours, mine, or Einstein's—there are no unused parts. None.

The myth that we use only 10 percent of our brain probably comes from the fact that much of the brain is not made up of neurons, the brain cells that are the basic computational units for thinking and remembering. You need more than neurons for your brain to work. You need other supporting structures.

Myth #2: You can damage your brain and it will still work

Correct. One reason why people may think that there are unused parts of the brain may be due to the early observation by researchers that damage to many parts of the brain did not seem to knock out brain function.

This is no longer believed to be true. Instead, researchers now know that the brain works through spatial specialization—meaning that different brain regions are relatively important for their respective functions. If the part of your brain that specializes in vision were severely damaged, for example, you would still be able to hear because hearing is controlled by a different section of the brain.

Myth #3: You can't grow new brain cells

Actually, you can—at least for some specific kinds of neurons in some particular regions of the brain. But equally important is the fact that you don't even have to. Research has clearly demonstrated that specific types of mental exercise can improve your ability to think, learn, remember, and make decisions, simply by rewiring your circuits to function more efficiently.

One example is a recent study on dementia, a condition characterized by an accelerated memory decline associated with aging. The researchers showed that study participants who took a greater part in cognitive leisure activities (such as reading, playing music, solving logic puzzles, and playing games like the ones in this book) were less likely to experience early memory decline.

Specifically, each additional day of cognitive leisure activities was associated with a two-month delay in the onset of accelerated memory decline.

Activities such as playing an instrument can prevent early memory decline, changing the neurophysiology of the brain.

Mental Exercise Changes Brain Structure

The brain is a fascinatingly complex, complicated organ, and—mostly with the help of new imaging technologies—we are only just beginning to understand how it works and helps us to get through the complexities of the tasks we perform every day.

Take city driving, for example. Some cities use a grid system; the streets in others can pretty much go in any direction. The names of the streets are just as arbitrary. The result is that driving around is a big challenge—to the brain.

Fortunately, there's a region in the brain called the posterior hippocampus, which contains neurons supporting this kind of spatial navigation. What's more, specific studies have shown that taxi drivers in London have larger, somewhat more developed posterior hippocampi. In one study, for example, researchers put taxi drivers into an MRI (magnetic resonance imaging) machine, which is the device that doctors use to take "pictures" of the brain or other parts of the body to check for anything from a brain tumor to a slipped disk. With the MRI pictures of the brain, the researchers were able to analyze the volume and density of brain tissue.

The result? Not only were the posterior hippocampi found to be larger in taxi drivers, the size of this region was also found to be correlated with the number of years that the person spent as a taxi driver. In other words, the longer someone had been driving a taxi, the larger the posterior hippocampi!

When you have such a dramatic demonstration as this, scientists are often rightly skeptical. Can this really be specific to the spatial navigation needed to drive a taxi in London? Could it just be due to the fact that driving a taxi requires a lot of sitting down, interactivity with strangers, and...driving?

Although all of us can come up with alternative explanations such as these, the researchers produced a pretty convincing follow-up study with stringent controls, showing that the effect is specific to taxi drivers, though not bus drivers. Bus drivers drive pretty much the same amount of time, except that it's always along the same route. They don't need to keep the whole map of the city in their heads.

What this proves is that specific exercises for specific regions of the brain cause that part of the brain to grow. But you don't have to drive taxis to take advantage of this function. In another study, using similar techniques, researchers showed that even learning

The brain is the most complex biological structure known to modern science. Despite advances in science technology, we still know relatively little about how this complex organ works.

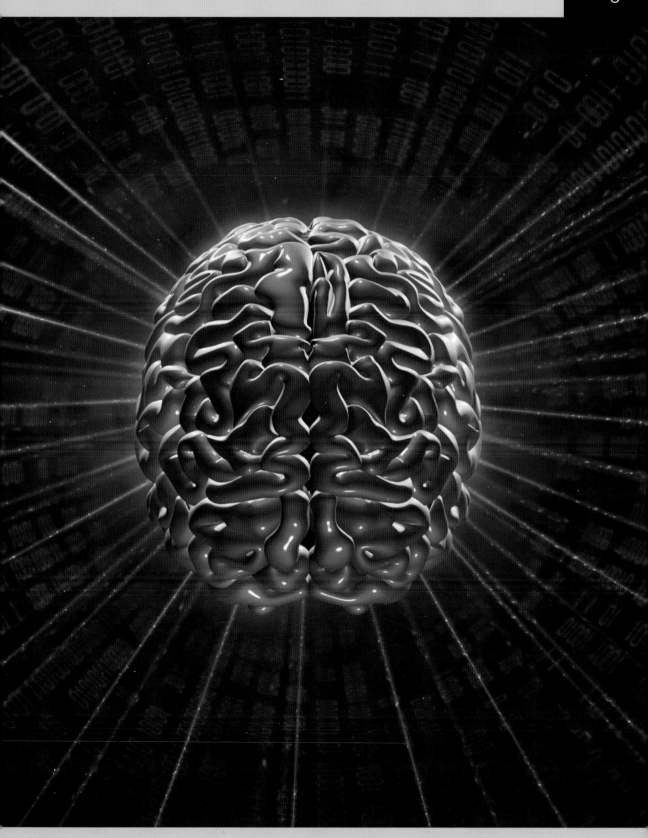

how to juggle balls can lead to significant brain changes observable by MRI.

In that study, volunteers learned the classic three-ball juggle over a period of three months. Significant structural changes were found in an area that specializes in processing visual motion. Amazingly, after another three months (during which the study participants didn't juggle), the researchers again took brain images of the volunteers—and found that the structural change in the visual motion area partially, though not completely, returned to baseline, the point at which it stood before they learned to juggle.

Clearly, the message of this study is: Use it or lose it!

Rewiring the Brain

Although training one section or another of the brain can increase the abilities managed in that area, many brain functions depend on the interaction of different brain areas. Different areas in the cortex are connected by something known as "white matter" fibers. In one study, for example, it was shown that structural changes in these fibers were associated with extensive piano practice, an exercise that requires the cooperation of many regions of the brain, most obviously between the motor areas respectively controlling the different hands.

Again, researchers in that study used an MRI scanner and took pictures of the brains of human volunteers who played the piano. The researchers used a special protocol called diffusion tensor imaging (DTI), which allowed them to focus on the "white matter" fibers. The intensity of the image of the fibers connecting the different regions was found to be higher in people who practiced the piano a lot. This suggests that these fibers were stronger, or better developed. This was particularly the case for young children, but it also applied to adults.

So far we have discussed examples that involve having some specialized training: learning how to drive around London, juggling balls, and playing the piano. But what about the more common mental functions? Can these be improved via exercise as well?

One of the standard tasks that cognitive psychologists like to use to test mental capacity is the working-memory task. Roughly speaking, working memory is what you can keep online in your mind. For instance, try to remember a new telephone number and hold it in your mind. You probably rehearse in your mind over and over again. The moment you pay attention to something else, it's gone, unless you have been rehearsing it for such a long period that it enters your long-term memory. It's not difficult to see why someone would prefer to have a larger brain capacity for working memory. Having a limited working memory is exactly the reason why we forget what we are about to say in the middle of a conversation—or experience other similar embarrassments in daily life.

In one study, however, it has been shown that a few weeks of specialized training can increase working-memory capacity. Amazingly, again by using brain imaging, it was found that there was an increase in the density of the brain's receptors for a major neurotransmitter known as dopamine. Dopamine has been linked to many functions related to reward, attention, and so on. An increase in the density of its receptors means the brain has improved its efficiency in making use of this key neurotransmitter, which in turn explains why such training improves people's working-memory capacity.

Training, which is essentially performing mental aerobics like the ones you will find in this book, could well prevent you from losing your keys, forgetting appointments, and overlooking your best friend's birthday.

So what are you waiting for? Turn the page and take the first step toward building a better brain!

—HAKWAN LAU, Ph.D.
COLUMBIA UNIVERSITY

> "Rest, with nothing else, results in rust. It corrodes the mechanisms of the brain. The rhubarb that no one picks goes to seed."
>
> —WILDER PENFIELD

One Day of Neurobics Buys an Extra 2 Months of Memory Power

A recent study on dementia, which is characterized by accelerated memory decline associated with aging, found that study participants who engaged more in cognitive leisure activities such as reading, playing music, or solving logic puzzles and playing games like the ones in this book are less likely to experience early memory decline. Specifically, each additional day of these activities is associated with a two-month delay in the onset of accelerated memory decline.

1

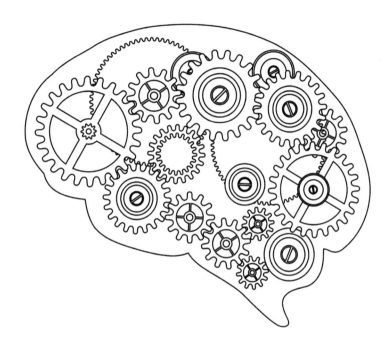

How Well Does Your Brain Work?

At its most basic, the brain is a mass of nerve tissue containing networks of neurons and synapses protected within the skull. At its most complex, it is a dynamic structure alive with thoughts, memories, and the knowledge of who we are. Clearly, keeping it in peak condition is a priority. But how do we know when it needs some help?

There are two things that can help us to decide. One is by understanding how the brain functions; the other is by solving a series of puzzles designed to test key brain functions in logical thinking, spatial awareness, verbal ability, numerical ability, memory, and creativity. Here's what you need to know.

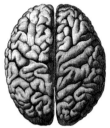

Brain Basics

For starters, the brain is divided into left and right hemispheres, each consisting of four lobes called the parietal, occipital, temporal, and frontal lobes. Each of the lobes is associated with a different type of brain activity.

The *occipital* lobes, for example, that are located at the rear of the brain, handle visual information from the eyes and the optic nerves. The *parietal* lobes, in the upper rear part of the brain, cover spatial awareness and different aspects of perception. Memory and communication, including language, are governed by the *temporal* lobes, located beneath the parietal lobes. Finally, the *frontal* lobes are the brain's "command and control" center, an area that governs higher and more complex types of brain activity.

In addition to the responsibilities of the different lobes, the brain's left and right hemispheres split brain function between them, although a vast number of interconnections enables them to cooperate whenever necessary.

Though similar in size and structure, one hemisphere is normally dominant in each individual. In right-handed people and even many who are left-handed, the left hemisphere dominates. It controls the nerves and muscles on the right-hand side of the body, leaving the right-hand hemisphere to control the body's left-hand side. Language and communication are usually handled by the dominant hemisphere.

Part of the brain's method for processing incoming information is to look for patterns to help it make decisions. The dominant hemisphere performs this function and also controls reading, writing, calculation, and the brain's perception of the position of the body and the limbs at any moment. The nondominant hemisphere deals with positional information, too, but is mainly concerned with the size and location of external objects in the immediate surroundings.

Memory is divided similarly: verbal memory by the dominant hemisphere and visual memory by the opposite hemisphere. The frontal lobes handle more complex proactive tasks, such as planning future actions, and learning and performing new tasks. They also handle drive and motivation and help control behavior and moderate negative reactions to outside threats or challenges.

Puzzles Can Measure Brain Fitness

All these complex and interlinked powers and abilities enable the brain to carry out various tasks and solve different kinds of problems. Of course, individuals differ significantly, and each brain will demonstrate lower or higher levels of efficiency in different areas. These patterns are revealed in a person's ability to solve the various kinds of problems and puzzles contained in this book.

When a person has more difficulty with puzzles calling for spatial awareness, for example, this may reflect limitations in that area, while a higher-than-average score in puzzles involving numbers could reveal a special aptitude in numerical ability.

This is true for all the main brain functions of logical thinking, spatial awareness, verbal and numerical abilities, memory, and creativity.

What kinds of tests reveal brain efficiency in each key area? Here's what we know.

Does Jack bark?

The simplest formal tests for logical thinking usually provide two or more statements or premises, and then ask questions based on those premises. Given the premises "All dogs bark" and "Jack is a dog," the question might be, "Does Jack bark?" On purely logical grounds, if both premises are true, then the conclusion must also be true. If, however, the second premise was that "most dogs bark," then the argument fails, since Jack might be one of those dogs that doesn't bark!

The advantage of purely logical thinking is that it doesn't need specialized verbal or numerical abilities to reach a solution. What it needs is the ability to think clearly and follow common-sense reasoning to move from the initial facts or premises to the right conclusion.

In terms of puzzles, logical problems may be descriptive, where the solution lies in spotting the fallacy in an argument or the danger of a false assumption. Let's say, for example, that a ship in a harbor

Fit Brains Last Longer

Increasing awareness of the brain's ability to improve its cognitive reserves—creating new neural pathways and connections to maintain high performance throughout your lifetime—means that brain fitness is no longer seen as a fixed asset determined at birth or in early childhood. By becoming aware of your individual strengths and weaknesses in the way your brain functions, and practicing to improve those areas that don't match up to your strengths, you have the ability to improve its performance with time, rather than having to manage with declining brainpower as you age.

has a rope ladder hanging over the side, and the bottom rung just touches the surface at low tide. If the tide rises 1 foot (30 cm) each hour and the rungs are 6 inches (15 cm) apart, how long will it take for the water to cover the three bottom rungs? The logical answer is never, because the ship rises with the tide, and the ladder will always remain with its bottom rung touching the surface!

Abstract logic problems often involve different kinds of series. These might be a series of words linked by their meanings, a series of numbers linked by their values, or a series of abstract shapes linked by the number of sides that form each shape or by the colors and shapes of symbols within the shapes. The object is to show the next term in the series. You can do this by analyzing the rules that link the existing items in the series and then extend that same progression once more to reveal the next item.

What does Jack see?

Determining how well your brain uses its spatial awareness to help itself organize information from your environment involves input from both sides of the brain—from the areas controlling the visual system, the balance system, and the brain's perceptions of the spaces involved in the individual exercise.

One common puzzle used to test the brain's efficiency is to scan a pair of similar, very detailed drawings and to spot the tiny differences between them. Common optical illusions can deceive the eye about what is being seen in a diagram—to decide whether a particular line is straight or equal in length to another line, for instance, when seen against a confusing background. Other tests involve deciding which of a series of irregular outlines can be pieced together to create a larger shape, as in a jigsaw puzzle.

Can Jack play with words?

Tests designed to reveal verbal ability begin with simple questions of grammar and word meaning designed to reveal speed and accuracy. Some involve looking at lists of words and suggesting other words with identical or opposite meanings. Others involve correcting spelling mistakes or filling in missing letters or choosing between words that have mostly similar spelling but entirely different meanings— weather and whether, for example.

More elaborate verbal challenges involve simple codes and cyphers, comprehension exercises, and verbal puzzles, such as anagrams or crosswords. Try drawing up a list of unrelated words and composing a sentence that includes as many of them as possible while continuing to make sense. Or try devising a code by changing the letters in a sentence from a newspaper to conceal the information it contains. Pick a descriptive sentence and try changing the picture it creates by changing the words used.

Can Jack add?

Numerical ability is another key aspect of brain fitness. Basic problems in mental arithmetic—addition, subtraction, multiplication, and division—provide a reliable measure of the brain's performance in this area. Others involve problem-solving of different degrees of difficulty. If one child in a family is three times the age of his or her younger brother, for example, but in a year's time the older child's age will be just twice that of the younger, it's possible to work out the ages of both children.

Other problems like this deal with the prices of different items on a shopping list or a restaurant menu; again, the trick is to use the information available to reach the correct solution.

Can Jack remember?

Memory is essential to all areas of brain function. Most basic memory tests use lists of completely unrelated words or objects and require recalling as many of them as possible after a specific time delay. A visual equivalent of the test

Basic arithmetic problems challenge the brain and measure its performance.

Verbal interaction is essential for keeping the brain active.

involves studying a series of detailed pictures. After a specific time limit, the test asks a series of questions about the pictures.

These memory tests have two important advantages: Unlike the other tests, they provide an objective standard of measurement, because memory improvement is evident in progressively higher scores when more words are remembered after a given time interval. Second, there are various techniques to help memorize names or facts, involving word associations, acronyms, and mnemonics, to create patterns and links to help retrieve the desired information.

Is Jack creative?

Finally, creativity is perhaps the supreme test of brain fitness, but by its very nature it remains the most difficult to assess and exercise, since it resists simple classification. It involves all the other abilities tested so far, and tests vary widely in this area. Most attempts to reveal creative ability are really tests of lateral thinking that call for a degree of inspiration to answer the question given, where following conventional methods usually won't work.

Here's an example where you're given a series of letters with no clear relationship linking them. You are asked

Creativity is perhaps the supreme test of brain fitness, but by its very nature it remains the most difficult to assess and exercise.

to fill in the gap represented by the question mark:

C R A A R I R ? I W A A G Y E

Applying the usual rules for solving a series puzzle won't work. Instead, this particular problem calls for an entirely different method—in this case, to look at words that might be hidden in the sequence. Some of the letters seem to suggest the word CARRIAGE. What happens if those letters are taken out of the series? The remaining letters are RAI?WA and Y, which suggests the second word contained in the series is RAILWAY and the missing letter is L. What looked like an apparently random sequence of letters actually contains two words written alternately.

Sound intriguing? Good! Turn the page to begin using all these puzzles to identify your own strengths and weaknesses—and build your own neurobics program!

"Elementary, my dear Watson!"

If you find logical thinking artificial and unrelated to the real world, try reading about an expert in logical thinking.

Closely following the narrative of a Sherlock Holmes story can provide dramatic examples of the value of logical thinking. Holmes's creator, Sir Arthur Conan Doyle, based his character's ability to read what can be deduced from subtle signs in a person's appearance, clothing, and behavior on the methods used by his teachers at the Edinburgh University Medical School.

2

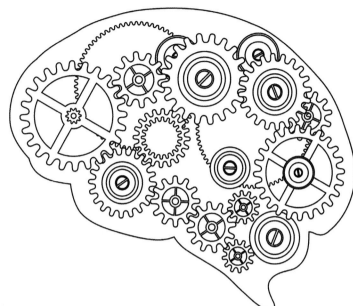

Baseline Brain Fitness

Before you can develop an individual neurobics program to maximize your brain's function, you need to check your ability in different areas. Once you can gauge how fit your brain is, you can construct a series of exercises to strengthen problem areas as well as maintain the brainpower you already have.

Test your brain's starting functions with light workout puzzles from each chapter. Are you good at logical problems but terrible at remembering where you left your keys? Are you great at sudoku but hopeless at crosswords? Do you have a gift for languages and words but are unable to parallel park? This chapter identifies your hotspots and troublespots and highlights the key areas in which you need to concentrate in order to boost your all-around neurobic fitness level.

Huh?

To test your ability to concentrate, for example, you can simply scan a couple of paragraphs in a book or newspaper and count the number of times a letter such as *d* or *y* appears in the passage. Afterward, write down the number of times the letter appears and try the test again. The chances are the answer will be different, because you may miss a letter you saw before or pick up a letter that didn't register at first.

This is because while we are reading printed text, we tend to scan words for their overall shape and context rather than letter-by-letter spelling. One recent experiment at Cambridge University, England, took a paragraph of text and replaced each word by an anagram, which is the same word with the letters in an entirely different order. The study revealed that when readers scanned the text, they could usually make sense of it if the first and last letters of each word were in their proper places, helping the readers to "see" the same completed words. Try it with the box on the right.

This piece may have needed deciphering here and there, but most words and meanings were probably very clear. Where the original words were not immediately apparent, the context would reveal what they were. This is why looking for individual letters is such a focused and time-consuming exercise, especially with letters that show up most frequently. As an exercise, check this

Try it!

Tihs is bcsueae in nmraol rnidaeg of pentrid txet, we tned to sacn the wdros for tehir olavrel saphe and centxot rehtar tahn tehir eacxt, letetr-by-letetr slepilng. One rcenet eperxminet at Cmarbgdie Uvrenistiy in Enlnagd, took a pargaprah of txet and rlpceaed ecah wrod by an agranam, wtih the lertets in an etreinly dfefrinet odrer. The sudty raeleved taht wehn rdrares snecnad the txet, tehy culod ululasy mkae snese of it if the fsirt and lsat lteetr of ecah wrod wree in tehir prpeor pcaels, givnig the ceuls the rdrares nedeed to "see" the cmoltpeed wrods.

paragraph for the number of times the letter *e* occurs, usually the most common letter in the English language.

How many did you find? Forty? Fifty? The correct answer is 62, and it's common for people new to this type of exercise to miss some the first time around. If your total was less than this, try again and see if you get closer. If it was more, check carefully, because this is much more unusual.

Do You Remember Mama?

Now let's take a brief reality check of how well you memorize facts and figures and the everyday details of your life.

Try recalling the order of letters on the computer keyboard without looking. Or try mental arithmetic by running through some basic multiplication tables: 1 x 3 is 3, 2 x 3 is 6, 3 x 3 is 9, and so on, right up to 12 x 3 is 36. Or work with larger numbers, such as 17 or 19.

This exercise also checks numerical ability. Try starting with a fairly large number, such as 250, and count backward by seven as quickly as possible, starting with 243, then 236, and 229. At the end you should be left with a remainder of just 5. Or count upward in increments of 27 until you reach the high 200s. If you reach 270, you're on the right track, but if the nearest you get to it as you reach this part of your series is 277 or

274, then you've made mistakes along the way.

Verbal ability can be tested by anagrams, especially those following a consistent theme. Check out the one-word answers to:

COLIC ORB
RICE CALE
DAMN RAIN
A CROSS EEL
O THICK EAR
IF COW LAUREL
ALPINE PEP
OMEN PIT
ERRS BY WART
TAPE SIGHT

Answers: Broccoli, celeriac, mandarin, casserole/escaroles, artichoke, cauliflower, pineapple, pimento, strawberry, spaghetti

What are the solutions, and what is the common theme? If these are too easy, use the answers to create more anagrams or fit the words into a crossword grid.

Try to memorize the letters on a computer keyboard as a handy brain-training exercise.

The traditional jigsaw puzzle is excellent for developing spatial awareness.

But Where ARE You?

Spatial awareness—essentially your awareness of where you are, what's around you, and your relationship to it—is more difficult to test. One way is to try mirror writing on a clean sheet of paper. Start with a simple phrase at first and hold it up to a mirror to see how accurately you have been able to transpose right to left the words you have framed. Or try it with figures, diagrams, or drawings of familiar objects where right and left are different.

Another spatial-awareness puzzle is the traditional jigsaw—even a relatively simple one. Fitting each piece into the overall puzzle involves comparing the small fragment of information on an individual piece to find its place in the whole picture, rotating it where needed to orient it properly. Pieces relating to similar parts of the puzzle have to be found so matching pieces can be fitted together snugly without using force. Finally, when dealing with areas of sky or sea and pieces of the same color, only their shapes enable them to be fitted together correctly.

Tell Me a Story

Finally, testing creativity requires a more unstructured approach. Choose some items at random from your surroundings, whether at home or at work or on the commute between the two, and devise a story to link them in some unusual way. Or watch the people on the bus, train, or street—which signs tell you the kind of people they are, what they do for a living, what their likes and dislikes might be. How could the information be woven into a comedy, a thriller, or a melodrama?

Test Your Circuits

Now it's time to use the puzzles in the remaining chapters of this book. At this stage, begin with the earlier and simpler puzzles in each section, because this is an overall brain fitness profile. Take the same number of puzzles from each chapter and note which types of questions seem easier and more straightforward to answer and which cause greater difficulty. Then check the number of puzzles you solved correctly in each category to see just how well your brain is doing.

In the most basic terms, score each test area as a percentage to give you the shape of your brain fitness profile. If you decided to tackle five puzzles in each area but have gotten one logic puzzle right out of the five, then your score for this type of puzzle would be 20 percent. If you solved three spatial puzzles correctly, then your score for spatial awareness would be 60 percent, and so on.

When you've finished, do not look at your overall scores but at the peaks and valleys. They illustrate your strengths and weaknesses.

Do you need to boost your logical thinking and verbal and numerical abilities? Could your creative or spatial-awareness skills be stronger? Was memory one of your low points?

Once you've identified your weaknesses, go back to the chapters to see which neurobics puzzles will give those weaknesses a workout. Start with the easiest problems first, based on your initial self-testing, and then move on to harder ones. Research shows that the most effective brain exercises are varied, novel, and challenging. Once familiar, they cease to stretch brain performance, so it's time to move on to harder problems.

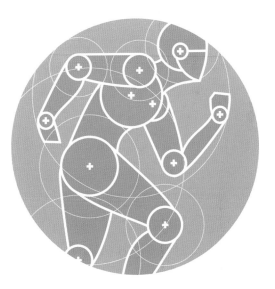

Use different puzzles from each chapter to test your circuits and identify your strengths.

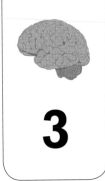

3

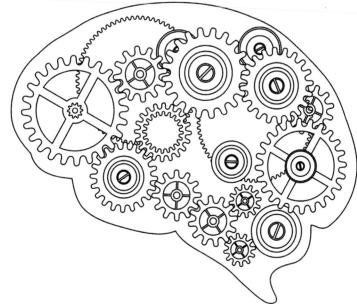

Build Mental Muscle

The best way to become expert at organizing information and using it to your advantage is to work at it. If your scores in this chapter suggest a weakness in logical thinking, you're not alone. Unfortunately, many of us find logical thinking intimidating. We see it either as a gift some individuals are born with or one that is acquired after years of study. Neither of these cases is true.

Though some of us find the process easier than others, thinking logically is an ability that can be learned and practiced. All it takes is common-sense reasoning, working from known information. Here's how.

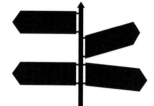

Look at the Conclusion

The simplest logic problems use a set of statements to decide whether or not a particular conclusion is valid from a logical viewpoint. However, most fall into one of several different types. Some pose an artificial dilemma that can be resolved only through logic. For example, imagine a traveler trying to reach an inn along a route he or she does not know. At a fork in the tracks, with no signposts to show which fork leads to the inn, stand two local bystanders. The question assumes that one always tells the truth and the other always lies. How can the traveler find the way by asking just one question?

Cancel the uncertainty

The answer is to find a logical way to frame the question, to cancel out the uncertainty over which bystander lies or which tells the truth. The traveler has to ask bystander A to ask bystander B which is the correct fork and then tell the traveler what B's answer is. If bystander A always tells the truth, then bystander B will lie. Therefore, bystander A's report of B's answer will reveal the wrong fork. If the reply from A is "B says it's the right-

hand fork," then the traveler simply has to take the left-hand fork to reach the inn.

But what happens if bystander A is the one who always lies?

In that case bystander A puts the question to bystander B, the truthful one. Bystander B tells bystander A that the correct fork is the left-hand one, but because bystander A always lies, he will tell the traveler to take the right-hand fork. So the result is the same: The left-hand fork leads to the inn.

In other problems, more complex variations may follow similar rules with more than two possibilities—the bystanders may be replaced by signposts that may be true or false.

Gnaw on a dilemma

Try to think of a variety of dilemmas that can be posed by different combinations of truths and lies and how the uncertainties can be eliminated by logic. How, for example, can the original problem be solved with three routes and three bystanders and different combinations of liars and truth-tellers?

Predict What's Next

Other logic-building questions can pose as great a challenge with a simpler theme.

These usually involve a series of letters, numbers, or graphic symbols, which change from one term in the series to the next. The task is to provide the next term in the series, either directly or from a series of multiple-choice possibilities. The solution depends on studying the terms used for the series and discovering the rules relating one term to the next.

Finding the rules

In the case of a series of numbers, for example, does the difference between one number and the next increase incrementally by adding another one each time (1, 2, 4, 7, 11, and so on), or does it double (1, 2, 4, 8, 16, and so on), or does it alternate between one and three

(1, 2, 5, 6, 9, 10)? Whatever the pattern, identifying it will reveal the next term in the series.

In letter series the characters may relate to their numerical position in the alphabet. Graphic symbols offer a wider range of variables but with enough examples to reveal the rules.

Look for the pattern

Sometimes lines and pointers within the symbols move around in successive symbols, like the hands of a clock, and sometimes other lines will complicate the picture by moving counterclockwise, or at twice the rate of the first set of lines.

In other cases, different shapes added to the symbols will also move

Some logic-building questions involve a series of letters or words that change as the series progresses. The task is to find the next term in the series, by discovering the logical rules that make one term relate to the next.

Logic can turn the information you're given into the answer you're seeking.

according to a different logical sequence to complicate the picture even more.

Finding this pattern reveals the solution.

Who Lives Where?

The third common type of logic-building question involves information relating to a group of similar people or places. For example, this exercise might relate to four houses on a city street, numbered 1 through 4. One has a slate roof, another a tin roof, one is thatched, another tiled. The front doors are each painted red, blue, green, and yellow. A mail carrier lives in one, a gardener in another, a schoolteacher in another, and a police officer in another. The question asks for the complete breakdown of which person lives in which house, with what color door and what kind of roof. The only information given is partial—for example, "The house with the red door has a thatched roof," "The mail carrier lives between the gardener and the schoolteacher," "Number 3 does not have a tiled roof," and so on.

Lay out a grid

The problem can be solved by laying out the information in a spreadsheet grid. Each column and row is named for a different item of information: the number

A common type of logic-building question involves taking information about a group of similar items, people, or places. Solving the problem involves sorting the information by dividing it into columns and rows.

of the house, the type of roof, the person living there, and the color of the door. All squares in which identical rows and columns cross are blanked out. Only where the information confirms a link between a row and a column are checked as correct—for example, the square where the line for "thatched roof" crosses the one for "red door." All the other squares in both the row and column involved can be crossed out as incorrect. Each fragment of information leads to more and more squares being checked or crossed out until the answer is finally revealed.

Set up similar situations

How can you practice this kind of problem? Set up a similar situation, plot the empty grid, and then work out the minimum amount of information you need to find the answer and how it needs to be split between the different categories. The more you practice, the easier it will be to solve more complex versions.

What Logic Does

Logic can't help you pick the right food to eat or the right beverage to drink—decisions like these are usually matters of personal preference. Logic can't help you decide the right course of action from an ethical point of view. It can't advise you on your rights and responsibilities or what you "ought" to do in a given situation—in a relationship or family dispute, for instance. These matters depend on different facts and different priorities from the mechanisms of pure logic.

What logical thinking can do is enable you to make decisions about what you don't know by working carefully and methodically from what you do know—and the more you practice logical thinking, the more your abilities will develop.

Work the Puzzles

In the puzzles on the next 18 pages, logic can turn the information given into the answer you are seeking. The key is to discover how the method works. Here's how to approach specific puzzles:

1) "Nuts & Bolts" (p. 32) and "Coin Conundrum" (p. 33) are puzzles that can be solved first by visualizing the information you are given. From here you can discount a number of probabilities and reach the answer through a process of elimination.

2) For "All or Nothing" (p. 34) and "Robotics" (p. 37) work through the process logically, stage by stage, to reach the answer. In "As Easy as ABC" (p. 38–39) the rules are clear—eliminate those combinations that break them and you'll be left with the right answer.

3) Other logic puzzles, like "Dastardly Crime" and "Aliens" (p. 40) are all about making an initial assumption and then testing it out.

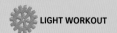

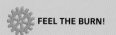
Logic Puzzles

Logic doesn't have to be intimidating. These puzzles will train your brain to approach problems methodically by canceling out the uncertainties, finding the pattern, and predicting the outcome. A grid will come in handy for some solutions. Read the questions carefully; all the answers are there in the information you're given.

1 A Special Date

The year 1210 is a special one in history. The first digit gives the number of zeros in it, the next digit the number of 1s in it, the next digit the number of 2s in it, and the last digit the number of 3s. The next such year is coming up soon. When?

2 Alphadigits

If different letters stand for different digits, and the same letter represents the same digit throughout, replace the letters with the appropriate digits in this (correct) sum:

$$\textbf{OH + NO = OHO}$$

3 Nuts & Bolts

You have three boxes. One contains nuts, another bolts, and the third one nuts and bolts. The labels have been mixed up so that each box is incorrectly labeled. You are allowed to withdraw one object from one box, but not to look inside or rummage around in them. Which box should you pick an object from to know which box contains what?

4 Going for Gold

You have three boxes. The contents are all as they should be, but the labels have all been switched around so that all are wrong. From which box should you choose a coin at random to maximize your chance of choosing a gold coin?

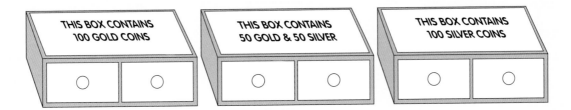

THIS BOX CONTAINS
100 GOLD COINS

THIS BOX CONTAINS
50 GOLD & 50 SILVER

THIS BOX CONTAINS
100 SILVER COINS

"Logic is the beginning of wisdom, not the end."

—LEONARD NIMOY

5 Coin Conundrum

You toss a coin a dozen times. If H stands for heads and T stands for tails, which of the following sequences is the most likely result?

1) HHHHHHHHHHHH
2) HTHTHTHTHTHT
3) HTTHTTHTTHTT
4) HHHHHHTTTTTT

Think Visually

Tackle a problem by conjuring up a vision of the information you're given—in the problems on this page, try to "see" the coin being tossed time after time and bear in mind what this involves. Or visualize the contents of the different boxes, and try out the effects of different labels on what seems to be inside—and what's really there. If Einstein could develop the concept of relativity by imagining traveling at the speed of light, the technique can work for you, too!

NEUROBIC TIP

6 Tim and Tom

Tim always tells the truth, and Tom always lies. Which one was heard to say of the other "That is Tom"?

One of them told me that the other had said, "That is Tom." Which one was it?

7 Just Good Friends?

Five friends quarrel, which complicates their planned night out. Charles won't go if Darlene or Abe is there, and Emma will go only if Abe goes along, too. Bertrand won't go with Darlene unless Emma is there as well, and Abe won't go if Darlene and Emma are both there. Which three get to go?

8 All or Nothing

A shuffled pack of 52 cards is completely dealt between you and another player. Is it more likely you have all the diamonds or none of them?

9 A Shifty Code

Can you decode this spy note?

**UP SFBE UJJT TFOUFODF ZPV OFFE
UP TJJGU FBDI MFUUFS POF MFUUFS
CBDL JO UIF BMQIBCFU.**

10 Decoding

Can you decode this spy note?

**GSRH XLWV IVKOZXVH ZMB OVGGVI
LU GSV ZOKSZYVG YB LMV ZH UZI
UILN GSV VMW ZH RG RH UILN GSV
YVTRMMRMT.**

SPY
CODES

Albert   Bertrand   Cuthbert

11 Identity Fraud

Albert, Bertrand, and Cuthbert all lie
about their identities. "I am Albert," says
the first. "I am Bertrand," says the second.
"I'm Cuthbert," says the third. What simple
question requiring only yes or no for an
answer could be asked of the third man to
enable you to sort out who is who?

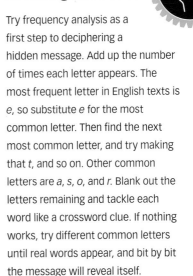

NEUROBIC TIP

Breaking the Codes

Try frequency analysis as a
first step to deciphering a
hidden message. Add up the number
of times each letter appears. The
most frequent letter in English texts is
e, so substitute *e* for the most
common letter. Then find the next
most common letter, and try making
that *t*, and so on. Other common
letters are *a*, *s*, *o*, and *r*. Blank out the
letters remaining and tackle each
word like a crossword clue. If nothing
works, try different common letters
until real words appear, and bit by bit
the message will reveal itself.

12 The Posse

The sheriff of Big Town wanted to raise a huge posse to track down the Guessy Games Gang. He decided to pick out 1,467 men at random from the available 7,614, but he thought that might be too few men and so he chose 6,147 men instead. Out of the available men, were there more ways to choose 1,467 or 6,147?

13 Hat Trick

A hat is placed on the head of two people in the dark, and the light is turned on. The hats were chosen from two white hats and one black hat and the participants know this. Each can see the other's hat but not his own. Once the first realized the second couldn't figure out his own hat color, he was quick to deduce his own. What was it?

Probabilities

Tackle problems where chance is involved by working out the probability of the different outcomes at each stage. For example, in puzzle 8 the playing-cards problem involves dealing 26 cards each to yourself and another player. Begin with the probability of your being dealt a diamond as your first card—then carry on with the second and third, and so on. But watch out for hidden traps. The robot in puzzle 14 climbs up 9 steps and down 5 steps, so that at the end of each move it is 4 steps higher. But what happens if on its final move it reaches the top of the staircase before moving down again?

NEUROBIC TIP

14 Robotics

A robot climbs 100 stairs in a number of moves. For each move, it climbs 9 steps up and 5 steps down, and each step, up or down, takes a second. How long does it take to reach the top of the stairs?

Reaction Times

NEUROBIC TIP

Logic skills require fast understanding and comprehension. Play a sport in the backyard to enhance your brain's reaction times.

15 Bad Hat Day

Four cops emerging from their police station are handed their four hats at random. Each one gets a hat but not necessarily his own! What are the chances of all four being allocated the wrong hat?

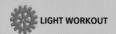  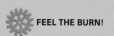

16 As Easy as ABC 1–6

Each row and column should contain a single A, B, and C. A letter given at the end of the row (or column) indicates the first letter encountered when you look down that row (or column) from the end of the row (or column) in which the letter appears.

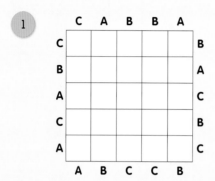

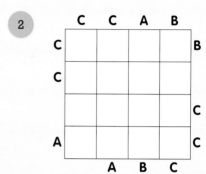

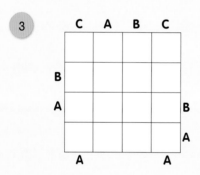

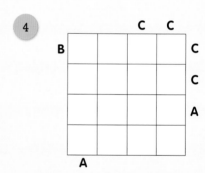

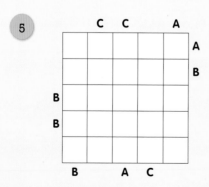

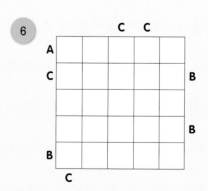

17 As Easy as ABC 7–8

Each row and column should contain a single A, B, C, and D. A letter provided at the end of the row (or column) indicates the first letter encountered when you look down that row (or column) from the end of the row (or column) in which the letter appears.

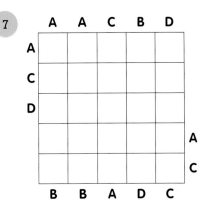

7

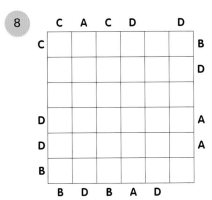

8

18 As Easy as ABC 9–10

Each row and column should contain a single A, B, C, D, and E. A letter given at the end of the row (or column) indicates the first letter encountered when you look down that row (or column) from the end of the row (or column) in which the letter appears.

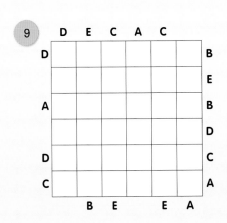

9

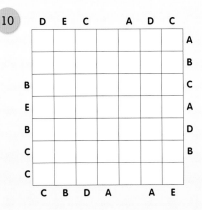

10

19 Dastardly Crime

Della did it.

Stella did it.

I didn't do it.

Della lied when she said that I did it.

Arabella   Della   Bella   Stella

Four characters, one of whom was known to have committed a certain dastardly crime, were detained and questioned by the Truthtown police.

Arabella said: Della did it.
Della said: Stella did it.
Bella said: I didn't do it.
Stella said: Della lied when she said that I did it.

a) Only one of these statements is true. Which of them is guilty?

b) What if, instead, only one statement was false? Who would have been guilty then?

20 Aliens

Venusians always lie, and Martians always tell the truth. Jack, Jemima, Jim, Jordan, and Jumbo are all Venusians or Martians. Which are Venusians and which Martians?

Jumbo is a Martian.

Jemima is not a Martian.

Jack is a Venusian.

Jim is not a Venusian.

Jordan and Jim come from different planets.

Jim   Jumbo   Jemima   Jordan   Jack

21 On Reflection 1

The word SHOEBOX (printed in block capitals across the page) when viewed upside down in a mirror reads the same apart from a single letter.
Which one? Why?

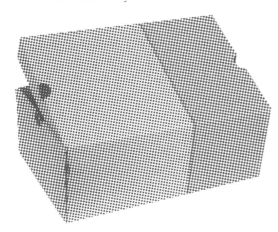

Step by Step

On the surface, the problems on this page appear as if they defy logic. But all you need to do to solve them is to make an assumption and then test it out. For example, in puzzle 20 all the aliens might be Martians, or they might all be Venusians. Assume the first is true, and check whether or not what they say fits the condition. If so, then that's the right answer. If not, then the other answer is correct.

NEUROBIC TIP

22 Card Shark

A gambler has a Jack, a Queen, and a King of Hearts face down on the table. He claims that the first card—the card on the left—is a Jack. He says that the middle card is not a Jack. He says that the card on the right is not a King. Only one of these statements is true. What are the cards from left to right?

JACK

NOT
A
JACK

NOT
A
KING

23 Three Cards

You are told that every one of the three cards shown that has a letter on one side must have a number on the other. Which of the cards would you need to turn over to check that this statement is true?

a) 1

b) a

c) ↑

24 Odd Consonants

You are told: "If a card has a consonant on one side, then it has an odd number on the other." Which of these cards would you need to turn over to check that this statement is correct?

a) E

b) 3

c) 8

d) B

25 Diamond

In how many ways can you spell out the word DIAMOND starting at the top and proceeding a level at a time and proceeding only between adjacent letters?

```
        D
       I I
      A A A
     M M M M
      O O O
       N N
        D
```

26 ❋ Route Finder

How many different routes are there from A to B? You may travel only north or east. One of the many possible routes is sketched out for you.

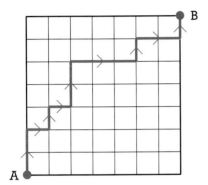

27 ❋ Ice-Cream Stop

How many routes are there through Abbotsford from A to B if you stop off at the ice-cream parlor at the intersection marked? As before, you may travel only north or east.

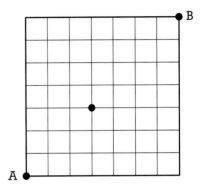

"Logic is the anatomy of thought."

—JOHN LOCKE

On Trial

Most of these puzzles can be tackled by making a choice from the options available. In the card problems, check each option and see which one best meets the conditions. In the remaining puzzles, note down the number of choices you have at each step in the process. The final number of options is the number produced by multiplying all of the different choices throughout the whole sequence.

NEUROBIC TIP

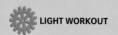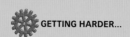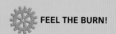
28 Hidden Treasure

There are three treasure chests in front of you, but only one contains treasure.

The label on the first chest states: "The treasure is in the chest that says, 'The treasure is not in here.'"

The label on the second chest states: "The treasure is not in here."

The label on the third chest states: "The treasure is in here."

Only one of the labels is false. Which box contains the treasure?

29 Captain's Cards

In a bid to make his authority seem almost magical, a pirate captain hands out his decisions using special packs of cards. In spelling out his decision, he places the top card on the bottom, then places the next card face up on the table. The next card is placed underneath, and the following card is laid to the right of the first card he laid down. He continues, placing a card under and a card down until the sentence is spelled out:

YOU*WALK*THE*PLANK

For this he carries in his ditty bag a special pack of 18 cards arranged ready in the right order. List the order of the 18 cards from top to bottom in this original pack.

30 ✤ Alphabet Gang

Four members of the Alphabet Gang were making their statements:

Ada: It wasn't Dirk. It wasn't Bobo.

Bobo: It wasn't Coco. It was Dirk.

Coco: It was Ada. It wasn't Dirk.

Dirk: It was Charles. It wasn't Ada.

Each of them told one truth and one lie. Who did it?

It wasn't Dirk. It wasn't Bobo.

It wasn't Coco. It was Dirk.

It was Ada. It wasn't Dirk.

It was Charles. It wasn't Ada.

Ada   Bobo   Coco   Dirk

31 ✤ Word Puzzle

What method must you use to decipher this?

Y E E I N S L
O D A S W I U
U T D D A N M
N O T O R C N
E R H W D O S

32 ✤ Every Second Counts

What method must you use to decipher this?

S A K B I C P D E F V G
E H R I Y J O K T L H M
E N R O L P E Q T R T S
E T R U T V O W R X E Y
A Z D A T B H C I D S E

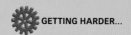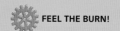
33 True to Type?

What method must you use to decipher this?

```
Rgw qies RTOWQEURWE ua ibw id rgw kibfwar qiesa
rglr xlb vw rtows yaubf kwrrwea dein rgw rio eiq
id rgw rtowqeurwe ibkt
```

34 Number Code

What method must you use to decipher this number code?

"4 84465 843733673 4 26" — 337227837

Handy Hint

If you can't decipher this quotation and its author, try texting a friend!

35 Simple Simon

On the way to the fair, Simple Simon gave away half his pies plus half a pie to the first person he met. He then gave half of the remainder plus half a pie to the second person he met. Finally, he gave away half of the remainder plus half a pie to the third person he met. As a result, he arrived at the fair without any pies. How many had he set out with?

36 ❋ On Reflection 2

The word **TOMAHAWK** written in block capitals vertically down the page reads the same when held up to a mirror apart from a single letter. Which one? Why?

T
O
M
A
H
A
W
K

37 ❋ Word Play

Identify the phrases clued here:

a) **GENE   RATION**

b) **THE HAND**

c) **NOOS**

d) **X☐**

e)  **BAKED**

"Logic is in the eye of the logician."

—GLORIA STEINEM

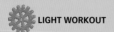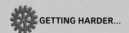
38 Fred and Ginger

Fred is 24, which is twice as old as Ginger was when Fred was as old as Ginger is now. How old is Ginger now?

39 How Many Candles?

The minister at the local church gathers up the stubs of candles and fashions them into new ones. He can make a new candle from 5 stubs. How many candles will he have the use of from a box of 125 candles?

40 Better Late Than Never

A man married his widow's sister. How did he manage that?

41 Decode

Work out the following statement:

ICI2IU

42 How Wide Is the Desert?

Three explorers set out to cross a desert. Each man has enough supplies to last for 8 days; that is the most a man can carry. They march off due east and keep to a straight-line course. After a certain number of days, one man goes back, handing over all his remaining supplies to the other two explorers apart from exactly what he needs for the journey back. A second man later does likewise. The third man just makes it to the other side with no supplies to spare. How wide is the desert (in days' march)?

43 Relatively Speaking

> I have no brother or sister, but that man's mother is my mother's child.

The statement shown is made by a woman standing in front of a portrait of a man.

What relation is the speaker to the man depicted in the portrait?

44 Bricks

A brick weighs a pound plus half a brick. How much does a brick and a half weigh?

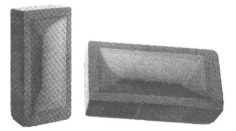

45 Clock Face

The clock face fell off the village clock on the church tower and broke into a number of whole pieces. It was remarked upon that the 12 numbers associated with each hour were unbroken and that the total of the numbers on each piece were all exactly the same odd number. Into how many pieces did the clock face break?

46 Step Pets

Work out the familiar saying:

STEP PETS PETS

1. 2020. If the year is coming up soon, it must be 4 digits long and must start with a 2. But if it has 4 digits, then the sum of its digits must also be equal to 4. (Note that this also applies to 1210). Since we already have a 2 and two zeros and we want all the digits together to add up to 4, the remaining digit must also be a 2; so we arrive at 2020.

2. The sum is 10 + 91 = 101; O = 1, H = 0, and N = 9. The sum of any two numbers less than 100 can at most equal 198. So the first digit of the answer must be 1, so we know at once that O = 1. So we have the sum: 1H + N1 = 1H1. Looking at the last digits only, H + 1 must have an answer ending in 1. So H must be 0. So now we have 10 + N1 = 101. This tells us that N1 = 101 – 10 = 91. So the sum can only be: 10 + 91 = 101.

3. Choose an object from the box that is labeled NUTS & BOLTS. We have two boxes, each of whose contents are unmixed. The other box contains a mixture. We are allowed to withdraw only one object, so we must be careful not to choose the mixture, because if we do, we will not be able to distinguish between the box that contains the mixture and the box that contains nothing but objects of the kind that we withdrew when we took one object out. Luckily we know that all three boxes are mislabeled. So if we choose the one that claims to contain nuts and bolts, we know the contents cannot be mixed. It is then possible to deduce unambiguously the contents of all three boxes.

4. From the box marked SILVER COINS. The boxed marked SILVER COINS is equally likely to contain 100 gold coins or 50 silver and 50 gold. So if you choose this box, you have a 75 percent chance of getting a gold coin. If you choose the mixed box, you will only have a 50:50 chance. If you choose the box marked GOLD COINS, you will have only a 25 percent chance of getting a gold coin.

5. Since an H is just as likely as a T, each of those results is equally likely.

6. Tim or Tom could say, "That is Tom." Tim would be telling the truth; Tom would be lying.
   Only Tim could say that the other had said, "That is Tom." He would be telling the truth about the other's lying.

7. Abe, Bertrand, and Emma go. Charles could go only with Bertrand and Emma. But Emma won't go unless Abe goes. So Charles can't go. Now, if Emma goes, Abe must go. But Abe won't go if both Darlene and Emma go, so Darlene doesn't go. That means Bertrand is the third friend to go.

8. If one person has all the diamonds, the other has none of them. So the chances of having all the diamonds is the same as the chances of having none of them.

9. To read this sentence, you need to shift each letter one letter back in the alphabet.

10. This code replaces any letter of the alphabet by one as far from the end as it is from the beginning.

11. Here's one possibility. Ask the third man if the second man is Albert. If he says yes, the second man is Cuthbert and he is Albert. If he says no, the second man is Albert and he is Bertrand.

12. There are the same number of ways of choosing 1,467 men out of 7,614 as of choosing 6,147 men out of 7,614. Note that choosing which 1,467 men to take out of 7,614 is the same problem as choosing which 6,147 men to leave, since 1,467 + 6,147 = 7,614.

13. The second reasons as follows: "If I were wearing a black hat, my opposite number would have known at once he is wearing a white hat, because there is only one black hat. So I must be wearing a white hat."

14. At the end of every 14 seconds, the robot has advanced 4 steps. After 92/4 = 23 such cycles, the robot is within striking distance of the top. This takes 23 x 14 = 322 seconds. After 8 more steps the robot is at the top, giving 330 seconds. This is 330/60 = 5.5 = 5 and a half minutes.

15. Consider officer A: There are three wrong hats he could be given. Then consider officer A's hat. There are three officers who could wear it. Once it has been allocated, there is only one way of allocating the remaining two hats so that they both go to the wrong person. Thus, there are 9 ways of getting it completely wrong. There are 4 x 3 x 2 x 1 = 24 ways of allocating them altogether, so the chances are 3 in 8.

16.

1.

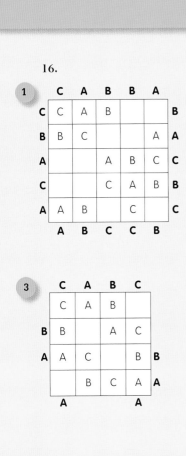

	C	A	B	B	A	
C	C	A	B			B
B	B	C			A	A
A			A	B	C	C
C			C	A	B	B
A	A	B		C		C
	A	B	C	C	B	

2.

	C	C	A	B	
C		C	A	B	B
C	C	B		A	
	B	A	C		C
A	A		B	C	C
	A	B	C		

3.

	C	A	B	C	
	C	A	B		
B	B		A	C	
A	A	C		B	B
		B	C	A	A
	A		A		

4.

		C	C		
B	B	A	C		C
		B	A	C	C
	C		B	A	A
	A	C		B	
	A				

5.

		C	C		A	
	C			B	A	A
	A	C			B	B
B	B	A	C			
B			B	A	C	
		B	A	C		
	B		A		C	

6.

		C	C		
A	A	B	C		
C		C	A		B	B
	B			C	A	
	C	A		B		B
B			B	A	C	
C					

17.

7.

	A	A	C	B	D	
A	A		C	B	D	
C	C	A	D		B	
D	D	C	B	A		
	B	D		C	A	A
		B	A	D	C	C
	B	B	A	D	C	

8.

	C	A	C	D		D	
C	C	A		D	B		B
	A	B	C			D	D
	D	C	A			B	
D			D	B	C	A	A
D		D	B	C	A		A
B	B			A	D	C	
	B	D	B	A	D		

18.

9.

	D	E	C	A	C		
D	D	E		A	C	B	B
	B	A	C		D	E	E
A	A	C	D	E	B		B
	E		B	C	A	D	D
D		D	A	B	E	C	C
C	C	B	E	D		A	A
	B	E		E	A		

10.

	D	E	C		A	D	C	
	D	E	C	B	A			A
	A	D	E	C	B			B
B	B	A		E		D	C	C
E	E			D	C	B	A	A
B			B	A	E	C	D	D
C		C	A		D	E	B	B
C	C	B	D			A	E	
	C	B	D	A		A	E	

(Continued on page 52)

19a. Note that Della and Stella contradict each other. So one is lying and one is telling the truth. That means that the only one telling the truth must either be Della or Stella.

   If Della is the one telling the truth, Stella did it. But then Bella is also telling the truth when she says she didn't do it. But only one of them is telling the truth, so Della must be lying. It follows that Stella is the one telling the truth and the other three are lying.

   Further, it follows that Bella is lying when she says she didn't do it. So Bella must be the guilty one.

19b. As in the previous puzzle, Della and Stella contradict each other. So one of them must be the only liar. If Della is the only one telling a lie, then Stella is telling the truth. Arabella and Bella, then, are also telling the truth, so Della did it.

20. We have to start somewhere, so let us suppose Jim is telling the truth. That means Jumbo is telling the truth, too. But Jumbo says Jemima is a liar, so Jack must be telling the truth. So Jordan and Jim cannot both be truth-tellers. Jordan says Jim is telling the truth, so Jordan is telling the truth. But Jim and Jordan can't both be telling the truth.

   Therefore, Jim must be lying and Jumbo is lying. Jemima is telling the truth. Jack must be lying, too. Jordan says Jim isn't a liar, so Jordan is lying as well. Jack is lying, so Jordan and Jim come from the same planet. Since Jordan is lying, so is Jack, according to what Jemima said.

This means we have four Venusians and just one Martian: Jemima.

21. The letter S. All the other letters are symmetrical top and bottom. That is to say, if you draw a horizontal line through the center of the other letters, the top and the bottom are reflections of each other.

22. If the first statement is true, then the second is automatically true. So the first statement must be false and, therefore, the first card is not a Jack.

   Suppose the second statement is true. Then the middle card is not a Jack either and the third card must be a Jack. But then the third is not a King and we have two true statements.

   It follows that the second statement must also be false and the middle card *is* the Jack. So the third statement is the true one. The third card must accordingly be the Queen of Hearts, and the first card from the left must then be the King of Hearts.

23. You need to turn cards *b* and *c*. You don't need to turn card *a* because if it has a letter on the other side it obeys the rule; if it doesn't, it is irrelevant. If *c* has a letter on the other side it falsifies the statement, so it needs turning.

24. You need to turn cards *a*, *c*, and *d*. You don't need to turn *b*.

25. Let's replace the letters by circles. You can arrive at a particular circle from, at most, two possible circles in the row above.

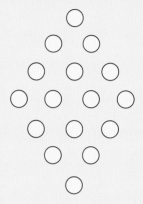

   Therefore, we know the number of ways in which you could arrive at the two previous circles. The number of ways to arrive at the target circle can be calculated by simply adding together the numbers in the two circles above.

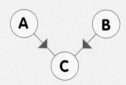

$$C = A + B$$

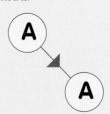

   If there is only one circle from which the target circle is accessible (because of the way the array is laid out), the number of ways of reaching it is the same as in the circle from which you reached it.

Starting at the top (where you write 1), the numbers in each circle can be filled in according to these rules, which should show the number in the bottom circle as 20. So there are 20 separate ways of getting there.

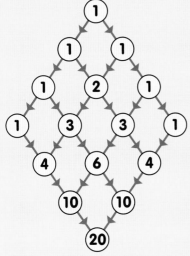

26. The same approach can be taken as with the Diamond puzzle. We start off with a 1 at A. There is also only one way to reach any of the T-junctions due north of the intersection at A, and just one way of reaching each of the T-junctions due east of A.

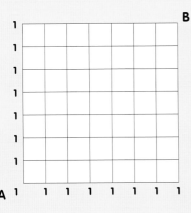

We can then start filling in the numbers of ways you could reach intersections adjacent to these T-junctions, noting always that the number of ways to arrive at a given intersection is equal to the number of ways to arrive at the intersection just west of it, plus the number of ways to arrive at the intersection just south of it. So first of all we get:

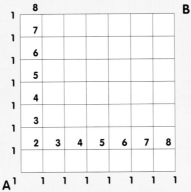

And end up with:

							B
1	8	36	120	330	792	1716	3432
1	7	28	84	210	462	924	1716
1	7	21	56	126	252	462	792
1	5	15	35	70	126	210	330
1	4	10	20	35	56	84	120
1	3	6	10	15	21	28	36
1	2	3	4	5	6	7	8
A 1	1	1	1	1	1	1	1

There is another, more abstract, way to get the answer. To get from A to B, we have to move seven blocks north and seven blocks east. Let N represent a move of a block north and E a move of a block east. So a typical route instruction might be:

NNNNNNNEEEEEEE or
NENNNEEENENENE.

The total number of routes will thus be provided by the total number of separate arrangements of 7 Ns and 7 Es in a line.

The number of ways to arrange 14 different symbols in a line is given by 14 x 13 x 12 x 11 x 10 x 9 x 8 x 7 x 6 x 5 x 4 x 3 x 2 x 1. That is because there are 14 ways of choosing the first symbol, combined with 13 ways of choosing the second, combined with 12 ways of choosing the third, and so on.

But the seven Ns are not all different! If they were, we could shuffle them to make 7 x 6 x 5 x 4 x 3 x 2 x 1 arrangements. The same applies to the 7 Es. The long and short of it is that 14 x 13 x 12 x 11 x 10 x 9 x 8 x 7 x 6 x 5 x 4 x 3 x 2 x 1 needs to be divided by 7 x 6 x 5 x 4 x 3 x 2 x 1 twice over, to account for the fact that all the Ns are the same and all the Es are the same. This, believe it or not, boils down to (14 x 13 x 12 x 11 x 10 x 9 x 8 x 7 x 6 x 5 x 4 x 3 x 2 x 1)/(7 x 6 x 5 x 4 x 3 x 2 x 1) x (7 x 6 x 5 x 4 x 3 x 2 x 1), which simplifies to 14 x 13 x 12 x 11 x 10 x 9 x 8/(7 x 6 x 5 x 4 x 3 x 2 x 1) = 3,432. However you get to the answer, it will be the same.

(Continued on page 54)

27.

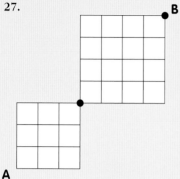

The route can be split into two parts. The number of ways to get to the ice-cream parlor is 20. The number of routes from the ice-cream parlor to B is 70. Because each of the 20 ways of getting to the ice cream parlor may be combined with each of the 70 routes from the ice-cream parlor to B, the number of possible routes from A to B via the ice-cream parlor is

20 x 70 = 1400.

1				70
	5	15	35	70
1				
	4	10	20	35
1				
	3	6	10	15
1				
	2	3	4	5
1	1	1	1	1

1			20
	4	10	20
1			
	3	6	10
1			
	2	3	4
A	1	1	1

28. If it is in the first chest, the labels on the first and third are both wrong. If it is in the second chest, the second label is wrong, and so is the label on the third chest. So it must be in the third chest. In that case the label on the third chest is correct, as is the label on the second chest, and only the label on the first chest is wrong.

29. YTOKUH*LWEANL*KA*P

30. Dirk couldn't have done it, or Coco would have told two lies: that Ada did it and Dirk didn't do it. But Ada says Dirk didn't do it (false), so when he says Bobo didn't do it, he is lying, so Bobo did it.

Checking this for consistency:
Ada: It wasn't Dirk (T). It wasn't Bobo (F).
Bobo: It wasn't Coco (T). It was Dirk (F).
Coco: It was Ada (F). It wasn't Dirk (T).
Dirk: It was Coco (F). It wasn't Ada (T).
This shows that the result is entirely consistent.

31. Read down each column in turn and you will get: YOU NEED TO READ THIS DOWNWARDS IN COLUMNS.

32. Skip every second letter, thus:
S*K*I*P*E*V*
E*R*Y*O*T*H*
E*R*L*E*T*T*
E*R*T*O*R*E*
A*D*T*H*I*S*

33. Replace each letter by the letter to the right of it in the row of the keyboard where it appears and you will get: The word TYPEWRITER is one of the longest words that can be typed using letters from the top row of the typewriter only.

34. Use a telephone dial to give you: I think therefore I am—Descartes.

35. Seven pies. The trick here is to run the action backward. In reversing a single encounter, we need to gain half a pie and double what we then have. Undoing the meeting with the third man, we retrieve half a pie and double what Simon has. That is (1/2 + 1/2) x 2 = 1 pie. So before the third encounter, Simple Simon has 1 pie. Before the second encounter, he has (1 + 1/2) x 2 = 3 pies. Before this, he has (3 + 1/2) x 2 = 7 pies.

36. The letter *K*. All the other letters are symmetrical left and right. That is to say, if you draw a vertical line through the center of the other letters, the left and the right are reflections of each other.

37. **a)** Generation gap
b) A bird in the hand
c) Back soon
d) Times Square
e) Half baked

38. 18. If Fred is *x* years ahead of Ginger in years, then when Fred was the age that Ginger is now, Ginger was *x* years younger than she is now. So Fred is twice as old as he was 2*x* years ago! So 2*x* years ago he was 12, so *x* is 6. So Ginger is 24 – 6 = 18.

39. 156. First he uses 125 candles. This leaves 125 stubs. This gives a further 25 candles. This leaves 5 stubs. From this he gets an extra candle. This leaves him with a single stub. This makes 125 + 25 + 5 + 1 = 156.

40. He married the sister first. He later married the woman he was with at the end.

41. "I see eye to eye with you."

42. They walk 2 days and the first then needs 2 days' supplies to get back. He hands each of the other two men 2 days' worth of rations, so that now they are again each carrying the most they can: 8 days' worth, and he sets off on the return journey. After 2 further days, the second man needs 4 days' rations to get home and before setting off for home he hands over 2 days' supplies to the third man who again has as much as he can carry: 8 days' supplies. The third man then marches for 8 days and after consuming the last of his rations, he stumbles out of the desert. If we assume that he gets full use of that final day's rations, he has been marching for 2 + 2 + 8 = 12 days, which is the width of the desert.

43. The speaker is the mother of the man in the picture.

44. 3 pounds. (Half a brick must weigh 1 pound. So a brick and a half must weigh 3 times this.)

45. The total of the hours is 1 + 2 + 3 + … + 11 + 12 = 78. 78 can be rendered as 1 x 78, 2 x 39, 3 x 26 or 6 x 13. If it had broken in two it wouldn't have said "a number of pieces," so the only possibility with an odd sum is 6 x 13. So the clock face broke into 6 pieces. This is what the division looked like.

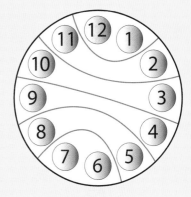

46. One step forward, two steps back.

4

Find Yourself in Space

Knowing where you are in relation to objects in your environment—what scientists call spatial awareness—may not seem like a big deal. Yet the ability is essential in every part of our lives, from physical activities, such as eating, drinking, reading, and writing to more complex coordination tasks, such as hitting or kicking a ball or tackling an opposing player.

What's more, it even affects visual memory, a skill that enables us to recall how things appear and remember information that is seen rather than heard. It helps us read maps and relate the information to our surroundings, and it involves recognizing shapes to solve puzzles involving hidden or interlocking images, or in reading a musical score.

Study, Compare, Ask

How do we improve spatial awareness? By studying details, comparing pictures, and asking ourselves questions.

Study complex pictures

One way to beef up your spatial awareness is to study two complex pictures—drawings or computer-edited photographs—that appear identical, then find the differences between them. A tiny detail will be present in one of the pictures but missing from the other. This means scanning each picture over and over, looking for those areas where an omission might be less obvious, since these are the most likely sites in which differences will be hidden.

Ask questions

Another approach is to study the pictures closely, committing the details to memory. After a given interval, you will be asked questions about the pictures. For example, in how many of the pictures was the subject wearing a coat? In how many pictures was the subject smiling or frowning? In which hand did the subject carry a newspaper? If someone were shown boarding a bus, what was the route?

At first these questions can be disconcertingly difficult—they reflect the problems many witnesses face when questioned in court over their recall of a particular incident. The police and other security services are trained to improve their visual memory, but these skills can be learned by anyone. Remember that the advantage of someone facing a visual memory exercise is that they know they are being challenged as to what they recall. People in the real world, however, usually don't know they are about to witness something important until it has happened. Consequently, anyone attempting this kind of challenge can concentrate far more closely for a few minutes than even a trained police officer on patrol through a busy city center.

Analyze what stands out

Tackle this kind of problem by looking for those details that enable a simple question and answer. Focus on colors of coats, whether or not scarves or gloves are worn, on jewelry, words and figures in signs or advertisements, on prominent features, such as eyeglasses, mustaches, beards, hair color, and so on. Always relate each picture to the whole series.

What similarities and differences stand out in a particular picture?

Practice

This kind of neurobic workout responds very well to impromptu practice. For example, while walking to and from work, try to recall the visual details of something that seemed particularly noteworthy at the time. Create a series of questions you might be asked if you had to testify in court. Then put the questions aside and study a few pictures in a newspaper before closing it and setting out to answer as many of the questions as possible. Here, too, practice produces progressive improvements and sharpens visual memory.

Work with Three-Dimensional Possibilities

Other spatial-awareness neurobics look for shapes and their properties rather than details in an overall picture.

Look for mirror images

A series of similar geometrical outlines may be shown at different orientations, rotated by different amounts, and in either direction from the original. The challenge is to determine whether any outlines are reproductions of the original

One way to heighten your sense of spatial awareness is to study the differences between two objects that appear identical.

shape rotated through different angles or whether they are, in fact, mirror images.

Look at the lines

A simpler challenge is to look at a complex set of straight lines that crisscross one another to determine how many lines are present or how many squares or triangles are formed by their intersections.

Or, given a set of complex shapes, figure out which of them are not needed to fit the others into a perfect square.

Define what's possible

Some spatial-awareness neurobics involve shapes cut out and folded into three-dimensional solids. For example, a set of six linked squares can be folded to make a solid cube. If each square carries a different letter, number, or symbol, then the task is to figure out which of a series of sketches showing several faces of the cube at once are possible and which are impossible.

And always remember that for extended practice in visual awareness, few puzzles beat the traditional jigsaw!

Work the Puzzles

The puzzles that follow include a wide range of different questions, so let's look at a few examples in which the methods suggested should give pointers to tackling others of a similar type.

Use your imagination

The questions concerning different markings on the surface of a ball, or the different surface pieces that can be assembled into a hollow ball (the principle is the same), call for imagination more than anything else.

Try relating what you can see in the pictures to the half of each ball you can't see and assume the pattern is continued on the reverse side without any changes or inconsistencies.

Slice it up

In questions in which material is removed from a block consisting of small, equal-sized cubes, the best method is to slice the remaining three-dimensional figure into a series of cross-sections, each of which is one cube deep. Then you have to use your visual skills to black out the missing cubes from each layer so you can work out the total material removed and thus the shape of the pieces removed.

Use logic

Other puzzles involve pure logic. The complex train of cogwheels meshing together in a circular path may or may not work in the real world. Try turning one of the wheels clockwise and then continue from one to the other, checking the direction of rotation. The second wheel must turn counterclockwise, the next clockwise, and so on. If the wheel that links back to the first one turns counterclockwise, all is well. If not, the geartrain would lock and nothing could rotate at all.

Pay attention to shape

Sometimes the shapes provided suggest the approach to be followed. A series of shapes divided by a horizontal line suggest that symmetry might be involved. Which complete shapes result if you assume that the missing halves of each shape below the line are mirror images of those above the line?

Questions that involve slicing up complex shapes call for logic and persistence. For example, a question involving a rectangle to be cut into two pieces to be reassembled to make a square suggests that the measurements given are crucial. Use the sides of the rectangle to calculate the area—the square will have the same area, so the square root of the area will provide the length of each side of the square.

Then all you have to do is work out how to make the cut to produce two shapes that provide a square of the right size. Don't forget to look for the occasional trap. When visualizing three cuts to slice up a cake into the largest number of pieces, you may decide that three cuts right across the cake will give you six slices. But if you cut twice across the cake to make four quarters, and then cut horizontally through the center, that will cut every slice in half at once, giving you eight slices!

Puzzles involving shapes are good for testing and improving spatial awareness; they often involve symmetry.

Spatial Surprises

There seems to be a considerable difference between male and female abilities when it comes to spatial awareness. In most tests, results for men show a standard deviation higher than the results for women. But that's not all. Results also reveal that women show a closer correlation between spatial ability and verbal ability, which suggests that their brains process visual-ability exercises differently from men.

Some occupations seem to even things out, however. Those who work in occupations calling for frequent use of spatial visualization—architects, for example—consistently show higher spatial awareness than people in other occupations.

Spatial Puzzles

Spatial awareness is a very useful skill, even for everyday activities like parking the car. Though it comes naturally to some people, spatial awareness can be learned. Practice is important, and solving these puzzles regularly will dramatically improve your power to determine distance, position, and movement in space.

1 One Ball

a) At how many points on the ball's surface do two seams meet exactly—that is, how many T-junctions are there, such as the one at T?

b) At how many points on the ball's surface do three seams meet, that is, how many Y-junctions are there like the one at Y?

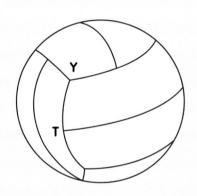

2 Soccer Ball

How many pentagons (black) and hexagons (white) are there on this ball? At how many points on the surface of this ball do three lines meet?

3 Star Ball

How many stars are there on this soccer ball? How many white shapes?

4 Block Cube

How many blocks are there in the stack shown? It originally measured 6 x 6 x 6, and you may assume that the only missing cubes are from the side of the stack that we can see.

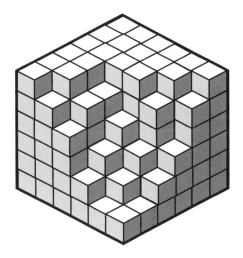

 ## 5 Cherry Cake

With as few cuts as possible, cut the cake into seven pieces, each with a single cherry.

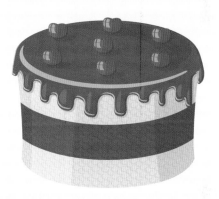

 ## 6 Plain Cake

With just three cuts, what is the greatest number of equal slices you can get from this cake?

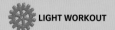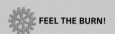
7   Cube Puzzle 1

A square hole 1 inch square is punched all the way through this cube in all three directions as shown. What volume is left? The cube measures 3 inches x 3 inches x 3 inches.

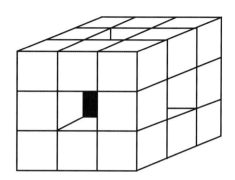

8   Cube Puzzle 2

A cross is punched out all the way through each opposite pair of faces of a cube as shown. This 5 x 5 x 5-inch cube was made by sticking together 125 cubic-inch cubelets. How many little cubelets remain?

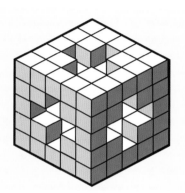

9   Cube Puzzle 3

A square, a cross, and a dash are punched all the way through at right angles to each pair of faces and all the way through a 5 x 5 x 5-inch cube, made of 125 cubic-inch cubelets. These show the views from each of the 3 directions. How many cubelets remain?

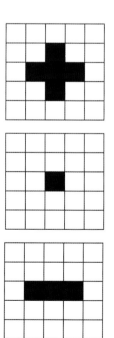

10 Fish or Fatso?

A fish? A pyramid? A fat person? Well, that's one interpretation. But what's the other, which will enable you to draw the fourth?

11 Fudge It

Divide this batch of fudge into two equal pieces by drawing a straight line through point P.

12 Divide Line

Divide the shape with a single line in such a way that both the blue background and the red rectangle are divided into two parts of equal area.

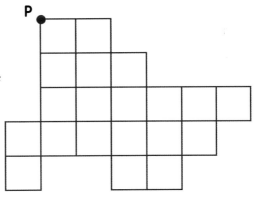

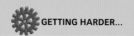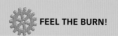
13  Cogwheels 1

What, if anything, is wrong with the circuit of cogwheels shown?

14 Cogwheels 2

The number on each cogwheel represents the number of teeth that each cogwheel contains. Once the left-hand cogwheel has completed one turn, how many turns has the right-hand cogwheel made?

15 Shape into Square

Cut this shape into three pieces that will reassemble to make a square.

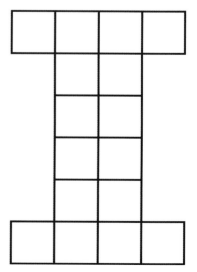

16 Three Shapes

How many different shapes can you make using the triangles and square below? They must all be used, and all must be assembled edge to edge.

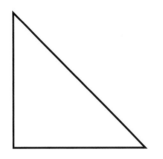
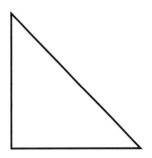

17 Flag Problem

At the first meeting of the Red and Blue Coalition Party, the design for their new flag was announced. All the lines are straight, and the diagonal is supposed to represent compromise. All went well until the question arose as to whether the area of Red was greater than the area of Blue or vice versa. What do you think?

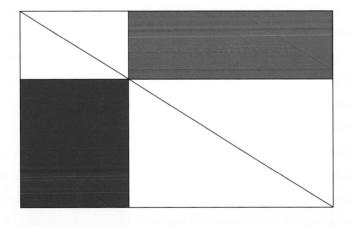

Have a Try

The best way to tackle these problems is to try them out logically. The first cogwheel problem centers on the direction of rotation. Start with one of the wheels and assume it turns clockwise, then the next will turn counterclockwise, and so on. The second one is numerical. When the first wheel has turned a full revolution, 51 teeth will have rotated against the teeth of the second wheel, which only has 16 teeth. This must have turned far enough for 51 teeth to have passed the meshing point. The same condition must have occurred where the second wheel meshes with the third. For 51 teeth to have passed, how far must the third wheel have turned?

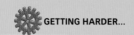
18 ✸ Triangle

A triangle is defined whenever there are three dots not in a straight line. How many triangles can you find in this modest array of dots? Count them, and then try to find a way to deduce the answer without counting.

19 ✸ Four Dots

Draw a square through the four dots shown.

Shapes and Sizes

Tackle the triangle question by drawing all the possible triangles in turn. By analyzing the method you are using, you will be able to find a way of working out what the total should be without drawing every possibility in full. In the squares question, do not assume that two of the dots lie on one of the sides of the square. As for the wine bottle, find the part of the bottle with the constant cross-section. Eliminate the problems at the ends, where this rule doesn't apply, by turning the bottle upside down and measuring what happens.

NEUROBIC TIP

20 Dr. Frankenstein

How can Dr. Frankenstein check if the flask shown is exactly half full, less than half full, or more than half full?

21 Bottle

How can you work out the fraction of the bottle that is left? Assume you have a ruler.

22 Freddy's Tiles

There was a box of identical tiles in Freddy's classroom. Freddy joined two tiles together edge to edge and got the shape shown on top. His classmate Emma joined two tiles edge to edge and got the shape shown below. Sketch the shape of the tile.

23 ⚙ Make a Square 1

Cut this rectangular card into two pieces that can be reassembled to make a square. The numbers give the length of the sides in inches.

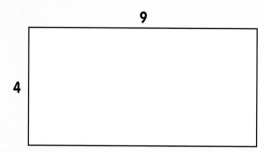

24 ⚙ What Pieces?

Cut this shape along the lines to produce three identical pieces.

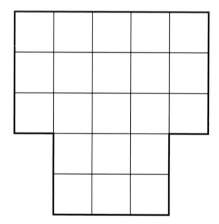

25 ⚙ It's Electric

The circled letters below represent electrical terminals. Connect the terminals labeled with the same letter without crossing any cables. Stay within the square!

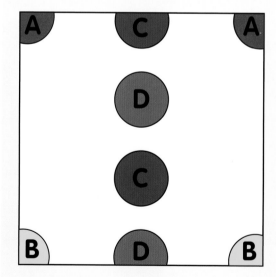

26  How Many Colors?

How many colors are required to color this picture if adjacent areas must be different colors?

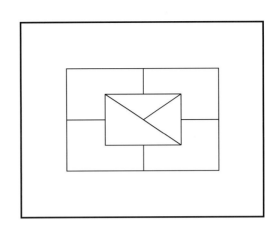

27 🌼 In One Sweep

Draw over the outline as well as the lines inside without taking your pen off the paper. You may not go over any segment of line twice.

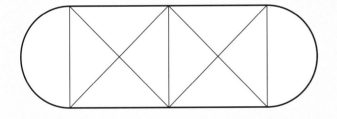

28 🌼 Haunted Castle

A ghost has been seen to travel from room to room inside the castle of which this is the room plan. It starts from the armory and passes through each segment of the inside walls once—and once only—ending up in the corner utility room. It never passes through an external wall. Where is the armory? At which corner is the utility room? Sketch a route.

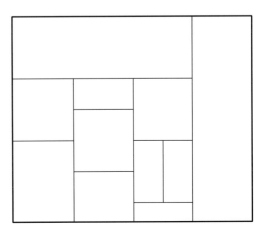

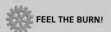
"There is no such thing as an object in absolute isolation."

—ALFRED KORZYBSKI

30 Papers on a Table

Eight thin sheets of paper—each a square the same size—have been placed on the table without interleaving. Label each one with the order in which it was put down.

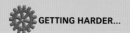

31 Terminals

Join the terminals in pairs of the same color. No cables may touch. Each and every square without a terminal in it must have just one cable entering it once and leaving it once. No cable may pass outside the outer square, no cell wall may be crossed by more than one cable, and cables can travel only vertically or horizontally.

29 Make a Square 2

Cut this shape into two pieces that can be reassembled to make a square.

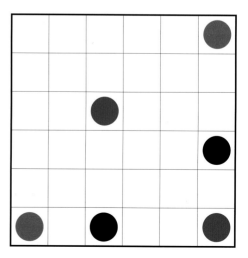

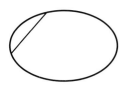

32 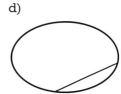 Optical Ovals

An elliptical piece of clear plastic with a line on it is turned face down. Which, if any, of the alternatives shown below represents the result?

a)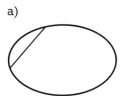

b)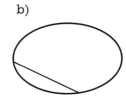

c)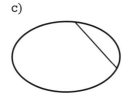

d)

33 Cut an Octet

Divide the L-shape shown into eight pieces the same size and shape.

Outside the Box

Don't get fixated on routine problems—improving brain efficiency means more than specific exercises. Try traveling to work by a different—and unfamilar—route. Don't visit the same places when you eat out; try different restaurants with totally different menus. Go to different places—even different countries—on vacation.

NEUROBIC TIP

1. **a)** Imagine the ball being squashed symmetrically into a cube. Then the arrangement of seams is as shown. The points—such as T—where a seam meets just one other seam at right angles occur one per edge of the cube. So there are just 12 such points.

    b) It is then easy to see that the points where 3 seams meet as they do at Y, occur only at the vertices, of which there are 8 in a cube.

2. If you focus on the black pentagon at the top of the ball, you will see that the seam from each of its 5 corners leads to another black pentagon going around the equator of the ball. There is another pentagon at the "South Pole" of the ball. This makes 12 black pentagons in all. There are 60 pentagonal edges. Three such edges are used in each hexagon, so there are 20 white hexagons.

3. There are 12 black stars. In between there are 20 white shapes. Do you see the connection with the ball in puzzle 2?

4. Think of the cube as consisting of 36 vertical columns of cubelets, some of which are incomplete. Write on the top face of the uppermost cube of each incomplete column the number of cubelets required to complete it. Adding these numbers gives the number missing from the stack.

    We see that this comes to 1 + 1 + 1 + 1 + 1 + 2 + 2 + 3 + 3 +

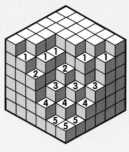

$3 + 4 + 4 + 4 + 5 + 5 + 5 = 45$. Since there were initially 6 x 6 x 6 = 216 cubes, there must be 171 cubelets left.

Whenever a puzzle offers a strategy for checking, it is worth doing so. The stack shown next is made by rotating the diagram so that we get a different set of incomplete vertical stacks.

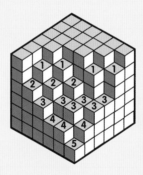

The numbers required to complete these stacks vertically give a sum of $1 + 1 + 1 + 1 + 2 + 2 + 2 3 + 3 + 3 + 3 + 3 + 3 + 4 + 4 + 4 + 5 = 45$, as we would expect, giving again $216 - 45 = 171$ cubelets left.

The missing cubes themselves can—by an optical trick—be seen by rotating the diagram yet again.

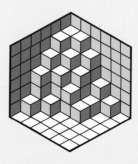

5. The cuts should be performed as shown. Unfortunately it is not possible to make all 7 pieces exactly the same size.

6. If two cuts are made vertically and at right angles to each other and the third is made horizontally and at right angles to the planes of the other two cuts, it is possible to slice the cake into 8 equal pieces.

7. There are at least two ways of solving this, which is useful as both ways should lead to the same answer. Checking is always a good idea when problem solving.

    In the first approach we imagine the shape that is made by the missing cubelets! We can visualize this as a solitary cube with an extra cube stuck to each of its 6 faces, making 7 cubes in all. So there must be 20 cubes in the shape.

    Another approach is more systematic and can be applied to the tougher problems that follow. Sketch out the 3 horizontal layers of which the shape is made. Then add up the number of cubes in each layer. The answer is, again, 20!

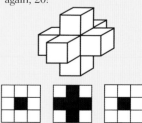

8. Taking five horizontal slices, we can assess more easily how many cubelets remain in each layer. In the top layer a) we have 20 left; in b) we have 16 left; in the middle layer c) just 4; in d) 16; and in e) 20. This makes 76.

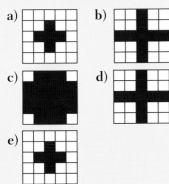

9. The pictures show the remaining cubelets in each of the 5 horizontal layers. In layers a), b), d), and e) there are 20 left. In c) there are just 8. This makes 88 cubelets left.

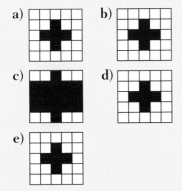

10. Each shape is half of the silhouette of a playing-card suit lying down: spade, diamond, club. The last one should be a half heart!

11. Rearranging the 2 pieces at the bottom-left corner and the 3 at the top-right corner, we obtain a 5 x 4 rectangle. This is easy to bisect: You just draw a line along its diagonal through P. But this line doesn't go through the two pieces of fudge we moved, so we can move them back to where they were without either of these two pieces crossing from one side to the other of the bisector. So we can bisect the original batch of fudge by drawing a straight line joining P to the bottom right-hand corner.

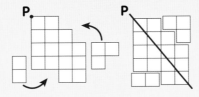

12. Any line through the center of the big rectangle bisects it. Every line through the center of the smaller rectangle bisects it. So a line drawn through the center of both rectangles will bisect both rectangles!

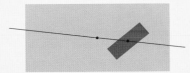

13. Adjacent cogs must rotate in opposite directions. If the topmost cog rotates clockwise, then going around the cogs clockwise from the top, the second must turn counterclockwise, the third clockwise, the fourth counterclockwise, and the fifth clockwise. But the fifth and the topmost are adjacent so both cannot turn clockwise! It follows that any simple closed loop of an odd number of cogs like this cannot turn! It is not possible to give a clear set of directions to the cogs that will not be self-contradictory.

14. If the left-most cog turns once clockwise, the middle one performs $5\frac{1}{16}$ revolutions. For each revolution of the middle cog, the right-most cog turns $\frac{16}{17}$ revolutions. It follows that for every revolution of the left-most cog, the rightmost performs $5\frac{1}{16} \times \frac{16}{17} = 3$ revolutions.

15. There are 16 little squares in the shape, so we are looking to make a 4 x 4 square. Cut and rotate into place as shown. Exactly 8 cubelets remain. How quickly did you find them all? Can you suggest names for the shapes?

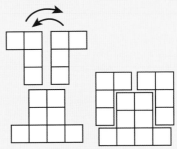

16. There are exactly 8, not counting mirror images. How quickly did you find them all? Can you suggest names for the shapes?

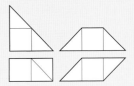

(Continued on page 76)

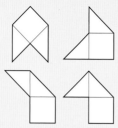

17. The diagonal cuts the rectangle into two equal parts. The areas on either side of the line are equal. The two rectangles are shared equally in the bisection, so the Red area and Blue area must also be equal. If you prefer to think algebraically, the lower triangle has an area $a + d + b$ and the upper triangle has an area $a + c + b$. These triangles are equal, so $a + d + b = a + c + b$. Therefore $d = c$.

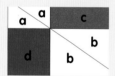

18. There are 76 triangles. Counting them all is a matter of being very systematic. The problem is, it is hard to squeeze all the triangles into one diagram. An intermediate method is to use labels (but you have to remember that we have to discount all those 3-letter sequences where the points are in a straight line).

    ABC
    DEF
    GHI

Let's list all those triangles with A as a vertex:

ABC ADC ADE AEF AFG AGH AHI
ABD ACE ADF AEG AFH AGI
ABE ACF ADG AEH AFI
ABF ACG ADH AEI
ABG ACH ADI
ABH ACI
ABI

Note that this can be achieved simply by listing all trios of letters in which the first is A. Within each trio we have listed the letters in alphabetical order. This is to make sure we don't get muddled and make a slip by including the same trio but in a different order. Seeing the pattern helps you to spot any omissions or mistakes. That is the advantage of choosing a system of labeling that facilitates the counting.

Similarly for B:

BCD BDE BEF BFG BGH BHI
BCE BDF BEG BFH BGI
BCF BDG BEH BFI
BCG BDH BEI
BCH BDI
BCI

The pattern is so regular that you should be able to write down the next ones almost automatically:

CDE CEF CFG CGH CHI
CDF CEG CFH CGI
CDG CEH CFI
CDH CEI
CDI

And so similarly with the remaining letters:

DEF   DFG   DGH   DHI
DEG   DFH   DGI
DEH   DFI
DEI

EFG
EFH   EGH   EHI
EFI   EGI

FGH   FHI
FGI

and last but not least:

GHI

If we count these, you will find we have 84 listings. But we must exclude: ABC, DEF, GHI, ADG, BEH, CFI,

and AEH and CEG, as these are straight lines. That leaves 76.

19.

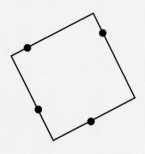

20. Dr. Frankenstein marks a line or holds his finger level with the top of the liquid. Then he inverts the flask. If the liquid is level with this line, the flask is exactly half full. If the level is above the marked level, the flask is more than half full. If it falls below the line, it is less than half full.

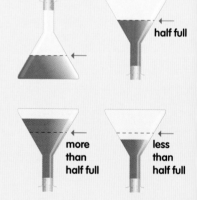

half full

more than half full

less than half full

21. Suppose the height of the liquid is y. The volume is $y \times a$ where a is the area of the cross-section of the bottle. When the bottle is inverted, let us suppose the height of the empty part of the cylinder is x, so the volume of air will be $x \times a$. So the volume of the bottle is $xa + ya$ and the amount of wine is ya, so the fraction of the bottle that is full is $ya/(xa + ya)$ or $y/(x + y)$.

22. We need to cut the L-shape into two identical tiles. We get the tile shape on the extreme left. A pair of these can be assembled differently to make the shape on the extreme right:

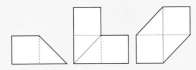

23. 9 x 4 = 36, and we are looking for a square of side 6. So we need to shorten the side that is 9 units long and add to the side which is 4 units long. Cut and assemble as shown:

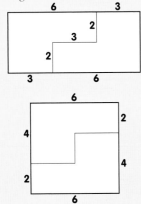

24. There are 21 little squares, so each component piece must consist of 7 squares. Note: one of the pieces has been turned over.

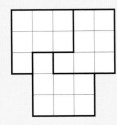

25.

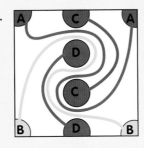

26. Four colors are needed to color the picture. Here is one such way of coloring it, where the letters *a*, *b*, *c*, and *d* refer to the different colors.

27.

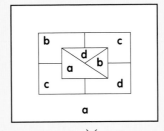

28. Any room that you enter and leave an even number of times must have an even number of internal wall segments. Only the starting point and the end point lie within rooms having an odd number of internal wall segments. The only two rooms that have an odd number of internal wall segments are here marked with an X. A possible route is shown. The utility room is therefore the room at the bottom left corner. The armory is the other room marked with an X.

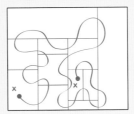

This is easy as long as you start at one of the two places marked with an X. Note that these are the two places in the circuit where an odd number of lines meet—known as a node. A node where an odd number of lines meet must be a starting or ending point. This is because INs and OUTs have to alternate. However, an odd number of INs and OUTs that starts with an IN must end with an IN (so we cannot get out again). An odd number of INs and OUTs that starts with an OUT must end with an OUT (so we can not revisit the place).

29.

30. Here is the order in which the squares are laid down. The first is 1; the last, 8.

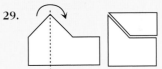

31.

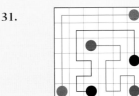

32. Choices b) and c) will both do (depending on how it is flipped). You can verify this by viewing the four images in the mirror and comparing the reflections with the original.

33.

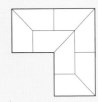

5

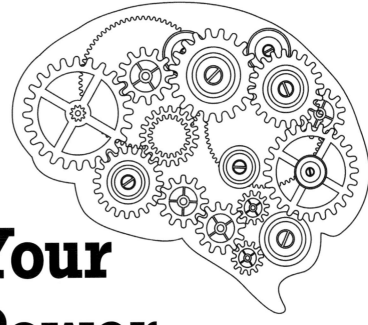

Boost Your Word Power

The biggest difference between you and your dog? Your ability to communicate through language. Verbal ability is one of our most priceless gifts, an essential tool in almost every part of our lives. If we can communicate our thoughts, ideas, feelings, and intentions correctly to other people, we can excel in our jobs, and have healthy relationships with friends and family. The ability to express clearly and precisely what we mean can help us win promotion and pay raises, make deals, win arguments, and gain and maintain strong relationships. Altogether, we can live a fuller and more successful life.

Verbal ability is born within us, but like anything this basic, it's easily taken for granted. Unfortunately, without some attention it will evaporate into a mass of unconnected words punctuated by *ahs* and *ums*. In fact, verbal ability needs constant training and practice to maintain it at peak fitness.

Use It, Play with It, Listen to It

Fortunately, whatever your ability with words, specific exercises can build and maintain the language centers of your brain. The key is to use them as much as possible. Reading a wide variety of material from newspaper features and reports to books of every kind helps improve the fluency and flexibility of the language we use. Listening to the spoken word—from friends and family, colleagues, professional actors, TV and radio presenters, and speech-makers—reminds us of

new ways to say or describe the thoughts, ideas, and opinions we need if we are to communicate effectively. But remember that language is a living thing, growing and changing from year to year, so look out for new ways of saying what you mean. And always practice, practice, practice, to keep verbal ability fresh.

Reviewing spelling rules

That said, there are specific exercises that can help, too. Spelling comes more easily to some people than others, but you need a wide vocabulary and accurate spelling to say what you need to while avoiding confusion. By

Extensive reading on a variety of subjects improves fluency and flexibility of language.

doing spelling exercises and learning the meaning of new words and phrases, as well as how to spell and pronounce them, you'll be improving the breadth and depth of your verbal ability. Most spelling exercises naturally tend to concentrate on words that are reasonably complex and habitually misspelled because of uncertainty over the rules. These help in learning where to use double letters, whether a similar sound when speaking a word is correctly represented by, for example, an *a* or an *e*, or whether a double vowel should be *ie* or *ei* in a particular case.

Because of the huge potential vocabulary contained within the English language, and the wide range of languages from which words were absorbed, learning everything by rote is too unreliable. Improving your performance in spelling exercises depends on learning the rules governing spelling principles, such as *i* before *e* except after *c*. This ensures that you manage to spell words like "their" and "receive" correctly. People with good visual awareness tend to do well on these exercises because they see the shape of a word rather than individual letters and can spot a potential mistake simply by its appearance.

Play with meaning

Then there are exercises to help learn the meaning of words. These usually involve selecting or providing synonyms (words with the same meanings) or antonyms (words with opposite meanings) from a list of words. Sometimes an exercise will provide a series of unrelated words, asking for the synonyms and antonyms in each case. In others, a series of words will require picking the odd one out. Anagrams—words formed from a word or group of words by rearranging the letters—are also popular, since this acts as a measure of the breadth and range of vocabulary as well as visual awareness.

Fit the words together

It's also essential to look at how words fit together into sentences to make a particular point, express an idea, develop an argument, or convey an emotion. Some puzzles provide a set of sentences with the key words missing: You either have to suggest words to fill in the blanks or choose them from a set of options. Other, more abstract, puzzles involve fitting a set of words into an empty crossword grid without any clues. The way to tackle this problem is to look for a word that contains an unusual letter, such as an *x* or a *z*. Since the number of letters contained in the word determines which spaces it could occupy, try out each in turn, and determine the influence of the *x* or *z* on other words that cross it. For example, putting the original word in one of two possible places might mean there must be another word with *x* as the fifth letter of 9, or *z* as the seventh letter of 10.

By checking the list of words to be fitted into the grid for words that fit the criterion in either case, it becomes possible to confirm where the original word would fit. Once this is determined, other possibilities can be checked out until the whole grid is filled.

And the wider your vocabulary, the better your performance at exercises like this will become.

Practice understanding

Verbal ability is essential to properly understand what people say or write.

Comprehension exercises enable you to improve this understanding by providing a paragraph or two of text and a series of questions related to the information it contains. These often ask whether a particular statement in the question is true, false, or impossible to determine. But measuring your understanding accurately means strictly limiting your answers to what the paragraphs actually say. For example, what if a question asks whether or not a particular animal lives in New England, and you happen to know that it does? If this is not clear in the text, then you should answer that this statement can't be confirmed.

Crossword puzzles come in almost every newspaper and magazine, and provide workouts to improve verbal ability.

Crossword workouts and codeword puzzles

What about exercises and workouts to improve verbal ability? Almost every edition of every magazine or newspaper includes crossword puzzles of varying degrees of difficulty, as well as the increasingly popular codeword puzzles. These have a grid of words similar to that of a crossword, but clues are replaced by each square bearing a number relating to the letter that occupies that square in the completed grid. Usually two or three of the letters will be identified by a number to begin with, so some of the words in the grid can be partially filled in. The resulting partial words may be enough to suggest the letters relating to the numbers in the blank squares.

Alternatively, counting the number of times a particular number appears in the grid can reveal likely relationships. If the number 7 appears most often, this might relate to *e* which is the most common letter in normal English text, and if 11 is the next most common, this may well be *t*. Similarly, numbers that appear least often are probably related to uncommon letters such as *j*, *q*, *x*, *z*, and so on. On the other hand, the compilers can choose words that modify the occurrences of these letters, and sooner or later an impossible word will reveal that a false assumption has been made. One way of confirming links between letters and frequency of occurrence would be to take a long section of text and count the number of times certain letters appear to see how consistently they occur in another section of text, chosen at random.

Tackle the Puzzles

Most of the puzzles on the next couple of pages are based on the exercises mentioned above: anagrams, synonyms, antonyms, codewords, and the like. But others tackle the need to get more familiar with a wider range of words by testing how one word can give rise to another by adding extra letters at the front or the back, or how one word can be concealed inside another, or which words can have an additional word in common to make a familiar phrase in each case.

Be ready, too, for verbal puns like the old one about four large capital *D*s, each one concealing a different letter inside it—first *W*, then *E*, then *S*, and finally *T*, giving the answer West Indies. Also, remember that adding commas, colons, and periods in the right places can change the whole meaning of a sentence. And don't forget the classic exercise of changing one word into an entirely different one of the same length by a series of one-letter changes, each time producing a different but recognizable word. All are useful for testing and improving vocabulary, which are vital to improving and maintaining verbal ability!

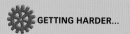
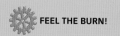
Word Puzzles

Verbal skills not only make you a world-class crossword puzzle-solver, they also help with general communication throughout your life. The problems in this section increase and test the power of your vocabulary as well as word recognition and understanding. The more puzzles you complete, the faster your brain will learn to solve them.

1 Home & Away

Change HOME to AWAY, changing one letter at a time, and with each move making a valid word.

2 Rearrange

On each line, rearrange the letters of the phrase to make a single word:

EAGER TUNA
AWFUL RECOIL
TINY CRUISE
EMPTY LEMON
TINY TOMES

3 Identify Word

On each line, rearrange the letters of the phrase to make a single word:

NINE THUMPS
HORRID CHAPS
PANIC ROOMS
MOUNTAIN COMIC
MINOR SPIES

4 Word Find 1

Identify these 7-letter words with the given last 3 letters.

****ARB
****CRY
****NIX
****RPT
****DNA

5 ✸ Word Find 2

Identify these 8-letter words whose second halves are given:

****POLY
****BOND
****NILE
****SAND
****BARD

6 ✸ Unusual Clusters

Find a word in each case containing the following unusual clusters of letters:

HUBA
GNT
PTC
NGPL
GGPL

7 ✸ Unusual Centers

Identify these words with the unusual centers:

RYB
LKM
LGR
PG
RSM

8 ✸ Sentence Fun

Punctuate these two sentences each in two distinct ways, one way reversing the sense of the other:

WOMAN WITHOUT HER MAN IS NOTHING

THE JUDGE SAID THE PRISONER IS A FOOL

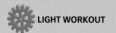 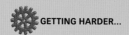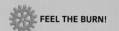
9 ❋ Word Puzzler

The vowel letters AEIO & U (not necessarily in that order) have been left out of the words below. How many can you identify?

PNDMNM
TPTNT
HSMD
DLG
SQ

11 ❋ On the Beach 1

Unscramble each of these beach things.

FOUR BARDS,
BOSUN CLERK,
TOWER COASTER,
SALTED CANS

10 ❋ Riddles

a) What do you call an Asian ox that talks too much?

b) Cyclops opened a school. Was it a big one?

c) Why is my amphibian so tiny?

d) What does a poor man have that a rich man lacks?

e) What do you call a penguin in the desert?

12 ❋ Metamorphosis

If FROG becomes **COLD** what happens to **FREUD**?

13 ❋ Word Thing

If:

ANY = COW
HOME = GOOD
CARGO = BASIN
NATURE = OBTUSE
CONTOUR = AMOUNTS
EQUITABLE = WHAT EDIBLE THING?

14 ✺ Evolution

Change DOG into HORSE in as few moves as possible with each move changing a single letter or removing one or adding one and at each stage making a valid word.

15 ✺ On the Beach 2

Unscramble each of these beach activities.

**BECOMING BACH
NUT BASHING
KING LONERS
ASPIRIN GALA**

16 ✺ Book Titles

Unscramble each book title.

**NATURAL DESIRES
CATHEDRAL LIONS
ONION OBSCURERS
THE SAILOR SWIMS BY
ON FINS**

17 ✺ What Links...

**ROSE, TREE, BOX,
ISLAND, DAY?**

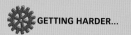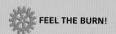
18 ✱ Lazy Spelling

Identify the word represented by the letters:

a) XS

b) SA

c) MN8

d) NRG

e) FEG

Sharpen the Focus

NEUROBIC TIP

Give your brain all the help you can. Try freeing your thoughts of all unnecessary information, and focus on the details of each picture as closely as you can. Choose the words that come to mind for each object and see how they work in combination to suggest the answer. If it doesn't work, think of other names for what you see, and try them out instead.

19 ✱ Down the Middle

Each of the words can be completed in the middle by another letter that will produce a downward word.

INS✱ECT
DAR✱ING
MAN✱GER
NEU✱RON
CON✱FER
TUR✱KEY
POP✱LAR
TRE✱BLE

What is the word?

20 ✱ The Last Word

Each of the words can be completed at the end with a letter that will contribute to a word that reads downward.

MEN✱
YOKE✱
PLANE✱
TAX✱
WAR✱
SULTAN✱
DIPLOMA✱
STAG✱

What is the word?

21 Odd Man Out

The words: HERITAGE, CIVILIZATION, PANORAMA, CHANNEL, and MOROSELY have a property in common. From the words in the following list, select the one that belongs in this set:

DECISIVELY

PROMENADE

MAMMALIAN

ELEPHANT

TIMEPIECE

LEMONADE

SAUSAGE

22 Lazy Spelling 2

Spell:

a) doglike (1 letter, 1 digit)

b) a country (1 letter, 1 digit)

c) intimate snack (1 letter, 2 digits)

d) ambassador (4 letters)

e) suitability for a given purpose (5 letters)

23 Dropouts 1

In each case the * represents a missing letter. Identify the words:

a) **C*A*N**

b) **F*A*T**

c) ***B*O*G**

d) ***P*I*G**

e) ***P*O*E*T**

24 Dropouts 2

In each case the * represents a missing letter. Identify the words:

B*A*K*E*R*

*T*R*A*I*N

*T*O*P*E*E

*B*R*A*I*N

*O*P*I*N*E

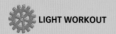 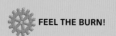
25 Dropouts 3

Replace each asterisk with a letter so that the sentences make sense.

a) The S*U*E*T was *G*O*A*T of G*O*E*R*.

b) The B*R*A*D gave me a S*H*O*E* of B*A*D*.

c) We ate a half-decent R*A*T and followed it with an A*P*E C*U*B*E.

27 Two-in-Ones

For each phrase below, give a word that means both parts of the given clue. For example: "only fish" would be "sole" and "observe timepiece" would be "watch."

a) expire cube

b) grumble fish

c) thump article of clothing

d) carry animal

e) animal edict

26 Seconds Out

Removing the second letter of the word to which the first word is a clue gives the word to which the second is a clue.

a) relative insect

b) pillages a great deal

c) make off with amphibian creature

d) display farmyard animal

e) shore composer

f) explosive insect

g) lecture fruit

h) amphibian mist

i) bird mammal

j) bore herb

Word Power

There are no single tips for these puzzles. What you need is as wide a vocabulary as possible so your brain comes up with the right word or words for each solution. So read as much as you can, varying the material as much as possible. And practice with crosswords or word-based games such as Scrabble or Codebreaker.

28 Homophones

Each of the following contains two clues to a pair of words that sound the same but are written differently (homophones)—for example, "unattractive fruit" would be ugly/ugli.

a) abandon pudding

b) island thoroughfares

c) set fire to Swiss town

d) part of the day belonging to us

e) gain seer

f) coarser dealer in miscellaneous household goods

g) poet prevented from entering

h) do smell

i) poison drumbeat

j) herb season

29 Beheadable Words

Each of the clues below refers to a pair of words, the first of which can be turned into the second by removing its first letter. For example: old story could be stale/tale, and record gibbon could be tape/ape.

a) intelligent crowbar

b) give birth to chess piece

c) country away from the sea

d) rinse combustion product

e) heavenly body drug

f) altitude number

g) more recent jug

h) fireside planet

i) particle cat

j) fragment object

30 Lazy Spelling 3

What's this? The number of letters in each word is in parentheses.

EZ4NE12C

(4, 3, 6, 2, 3)

31  Menagerie

Suggest an animal to continue this sequence:

ALLIGATOR, GIRAFFE, ARMADILLO, DROMEDARY, ELK, LEOPARD, PANTHER, TIGER...

32 Word Play 1

OAFS becomes UGLY, and LION becomes ROUT. What becomes LAYOUT?

> "Words without thoughts never to heaven go."
>
> —WILLIAM SHAKESPEARE

33 Word Play 2

In each of these words, the asterisk represents the same missing chunk. Identify the words:

BU*D
CU*D
MU*D

34 Triptychs

Each trio of clues is satisfied by a single word (the number of letters in each answer is listed at right).

a) Sausage, firework, car (6)

b) Sportsmen, garments, dogs (6)

c) Garment, films, electrical faults (6)

d) Rosebuds, errors, underwear (8)

e) Biscuit, drink, or rule (7)

35  Holes in the Middle

Into what four-letter word may L, M, N, P, and S all be separately inserted to make a new word?

```
— — L — —
— — M — —
— — N — —
— — P — —
— — S — —
```

36 Islands

Identify these two islands differing in their second letters only:

*R*****

*C*****

37 Riddles

a) What did the hat say to the hat stand?

b) What do you call a cowboy with paper trousers?

c) Where should you take a sick ship?

d) Why are cows so bad at football?

e) Why is a sponge cake like the sun?

38 Word Square 1

The letters of each word clued in this word square are all to be found in the phrase CART SLED.

1	2	3	4
2			
3			
4			

Clues Across & Down

1) Chemical—oddly scarlet

2) Top fliers—they could be high!

3) New deal for Zeus's conquest

4) Ruler of plastic arts

39 Word Square 2

The letters of each word clued in this word square are all found in the phrase TWO NEPHEWS.

1	2	3	4
2			
3			
4			

Clues Across & Down

1) All of, or the first half of, *Showboat*

2) Optimism of Schopenhauer

3) Frank love by enclosure

4) Departed initially from what Elgar named Titania

"What's another word for Thesaurus?"

—STEPHEN WRIGHT

40 Enigma

"Root or insect"—so say the letters of the word;
And yet 'tis neither, for it names a bird.

(9 letters)

41 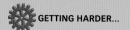 How Many Words?

How many words of 3 letters or more can you find in the word:

ENIGMATIC

Keep Moving

Staying in one place often slows down thinking. If you have to sit down to tackle a problem, don't slump. Sit up straight and stay focused. If you get stuck, go sit somewhere else for a while. Or go out for a walk, see a movie, meet friends. Chances are, when you return to the problem, you'll see it differently.

NEUROBIC TIP

42 ## Stabling the Horse

Take HORSE to STABLE in as few moves as possible, with each move changing a single letter or removing one or adding one and at each stage making a valid word.

 43 ## Word Square 3

The letters of each word clued in this word square are all found in the phrase OK FOR BEEPS.

1	2	3	4
2			
3			
4			

Clues Across & Down

1) Utensil in road?

2) Instrument—half trombone

3) Got up flower

4) Retain part of castle

 44 ## Enigma 1

Strike out the middle letter of something found underwater (5) to get something found underground (4).

 45 ## Enigma 2

A fish within a pig? Absurd! Denoting as it does—a bird.
(7 letters)

1. Here is one way: HOME, COME, CORE, WORE, WIRE, WIRY, AIRY, AWRY, AWAY. There are others!

2. GUARANTEE
   CAULIFLOWER
   INSECURITY
   EMPLOYMENT
   TESTIMONY

3. PUNISHMENT
   HARPSICHORD
   COMPARISON
   COMMUNICATION
   PERMISSION

4. rhubARB, mimiCRY, phoeNIX, exceRPT, and echiDNA

5. monoPOLY, vagaBOND, juveNILE, thouSAND and scabBARD

6. rHUBArb, sovereiGNTy, bankruPTCy, gaNGPlank, and eGGPLant

7. eveRYBody, waLKMan, piLGRim, poPGun, and oaRSMan

8. Woman, without her man, is nothing. OR: Woman! Without her, man is nothing

   The judge said, "The prisoner is a fool." OR: The "judge," said the prisoner, "is a fool."

9. PANDEMONIUM, OUTPATIENT, HOUSEMAID, DIALOGUE, SEQUOIA

10. a) A yakety yak
    b) No. He had only one pupil.
    c) Because it's my newt (minute).
    d) Nothing
    e) Lost

11. SURFBOARD, SUNBLOCKER, WATER SCOOTER, SANDCASTLE

12. FREUD turns into COBRA (shift each letter in each case 3 letters back in the alphabet).

13. FRUITCAKE. (The two words in each pair have identical text equivalents. So ANY = 269 = COW; HOME = 4663 = GOOD; CARGO = 22746 = BASIN; NATURE = 628873 = OBTUSE; CONTOUR = 2668687 = AMOUNTS. The (edible) equivalent of EQUITABLE = 378482253 = FRUITCAKE.

14. E.g., DOG, DOE, DOSE, HOSE, HORSE

15. BEACHCOMBING, SUNBATHING, SNORKELING, PARASAILING

16. Books about islands and castaways

    TREASURE ISLAND
    THE CORAL ISLAND
    ROBINSON CRUSOE
    THE SWISS FAMILY
       ROBINSON

17. Each word may be preceded by CHRISTMAS.

18. a) excess
    b) essay
    c) emanate
    d) energy
    e) effigy

19. PLATINUM

    INSPECT
    DARLING
    MANAGER
    NEUTRON
    CONIFER
    TURNKEY
    POPULAR
    TREMBLE

20. ULTIMATE

    MENU
    YOKEL
    PLANET
    TAXI
    WARM
    SULTANA
    DIPLOMAT
    STAGE

21. LEMONADE (Each word contains a girl's name at the center: heRITAge, civiLIZAtion, paNORAma, chANNel, and moROSEly)

22. a) K9 (canine)
    b) Q8 (Kuwait)
    c) T42 (tea for two)
    d) XLNC (excellency)
    e) XPDNC (expediency)

23. a) CHAIN
    b) FEAST
    c) OBLONG
    d) SPRING
    e) OPPONENT

24. a) BLACKBERRY
    b) STARVATION
    c) ATMOSPHERE
    d) ABERATION
    e) COMPLIANCE

25. a) The STUDENT was IGNORANT of geometry
    b) The BARMAID gave me a SCHOONER of BRANDY.
    c) We ate a half-decent ROAST and followed it with an APPLE CRUMBLE.

26. a) AUNT, ANT
    b) LOOTS, LOTS
    c) STEAL, SEAL
    d) SHOW, SOW
    e) BEACH, BACH
    f) THERMITE, TERMITE
    g) PREACH, PEACH
    h) FROG, FOG

i) CROW, COW

j) DRILL, DILL

27. a) die

b) carp

c) sock

d) bear

e) bull

28. a) DESERT, DESSERT

b) RHODES, ROADS

c) BURN, BERNE

d) HOUR, OUR

e) PROFIT, PROPHET

f) GROSSER, GROCER

g) BARD, BARRED

h) WREAK, REEK

i) TOXIN, TOCSIN

j) THYME, TIME

29. a) CLEVER, LEVER

b) SPAWN, PAWN

c) FINLAND, INLAND

d) WASH, ASH

e) ASTEROID, STEROID

f) HEIGHT, EIGHT

g) NEWER, EWER

h) HEARTH, EARTH

i) ATOM, TOM

j) PARTICLE, ARTICLE

30. It's "easy for anyone to see."

31. The name of each successive animal starts with the middle letter of the animal before: alliGator, girAffe, armaDillo, dromEdary, eLk, leoPard, panTher, tiGer

The next animal could be a new one, e.g., goat, or it could loop back to giraffe again

32. If you shift each letter of OAFS 6 letters further on through the alphabet, you get UGLY. Similarly LION becomes ROUT. The word that becomes LAYOUT is FUSION. It can be found by

shifting each letter 6 letters back in the alphabet

33. buSTARd, cuSTARd, muSTARd

34. a) banger

b) boxers

c) shorts

d) bloomers

e) Bourbon

35. HOES

36. IRELAND, ICELAND

37. a) You stay there, I'll go on ahead.

b) Russell (rustle)

c) The doc's (docks)

d) They have two left feet

e) It's light when it rises

38.

S	A	L	T
A	C	E	S
L	E	D	A
T	S	A	R

Notes:

1. Take the odd letters of SCARLET to give SALT.

2. Aces high is a set phrase and aces are top fliers.

3. New DEAL suggests rearranging the letters to give LEDA, who was Zeus's conquest.

4. Arrangement of ARTS gives TSAR — a Russian ruler.

39.

S	H	O	W
H	O	P	E
O	P	E	N
W	E	N	T

Notes:

1. SHOW is the first half of

SHOWboat; but it is also the whole thing.

2. HOPE is found in the letters of SCHOPENHAUER.

3. love=0 (as in tennis) + pen (enclosure) gives OPEN=frank.

4. Taking the initials of the phrase "what Elgar named Titania" we get WENT.

40. CORMORANT

41. 25 words: FAIR
50 words: GOOD
75 words: EXCELLENT

ace, act, age, aim, ant, ate, cam, can, cat, eat, eta, gem, get, gin, ice, man, mat, men, met, nag, net, nit, tag, tan, tea, ten, tic, tie, tin, acme, acne, amen, ante, anti, cage, came, cane, cant, cent, cite, emit, gain, gait, game, gate, gent, gnat, item, mien, mine, mini, mane, mate, mean, meat, meta, mica, mice, mien, mine, mini, mint, mite, name, neat, nice, tame, tang, team, time, tine, agent, antic, enact, gaming, genii, giant, icing, image, magic, mange, manic, meant, mince, tinge, acting, aiming, anemic, cinema, citing, eating, enigma, ignite, incite, inmate, magnet, mantic, mating, meeting, taming, timing, imagine, teaming, magnetic

42. E.g., HORSE, HOSE, HOLE, SOLE, SALE, STALE, STABLE

43.

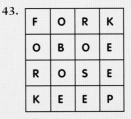

F	O	R	K
O	B	O	E
R	O	S	E
K	E	E	P

44. CORAL − R = COAL

45. sPARRow. A parr is a young salmon.

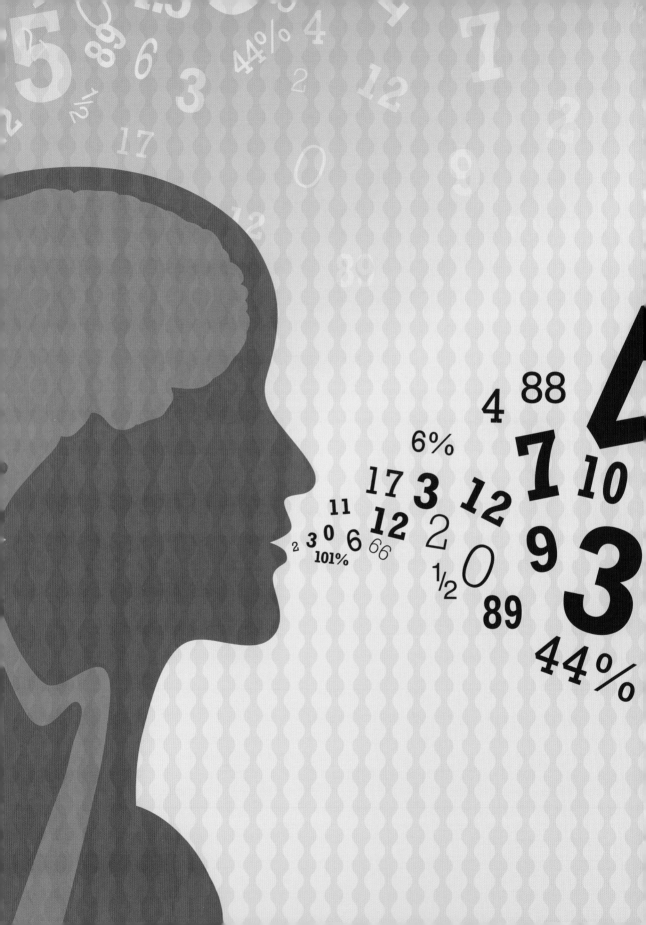

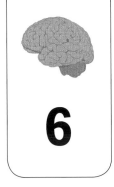

6

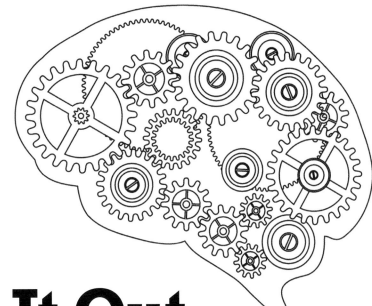

Figure It Out

Will you end up with more money if you (a) take out a home equity loan to pay for your kid's $114,000 college education or (b) cash in your 401(k)? How much of a tip should you leave the waiter on a $267.84 bill? Is it cheaper to buy green beans at the market for $2.89 a pound ($5.89 a kilogram)—or to grow them yourself when seeds are $3.29 for a packet of 50 and an organic fish-based fertilizer costs $23.99 a quart or liter?

Math is about life. And your ability to survive and thrive is frequently dependent on your ability to manipulate numbers. Yet many of us—particularly those who may have had problems coping with math in school—have a deep aversion to numerical questions. We avoid them whenever possible, which eventually leads us to lose even the limited ability we had to add 2 + 2 and come up with 4.

Rebuild Your Skills

Fortunately, it's never too late to put things right.

Math depends entirely on logic, and if you can develop the "hold that thought" needed to solve mathematical exercises, and improve your ability by repeated practice, then you'll find confidence and pleasure in seeing your ability and performance improve.

Start with the basics

Start with computation—using the basic techniques of arithmetic, including addition, subtraction, multiplication, and division, together with slightly more complex routines such as decimals and fractions, ratios, and percentages.

For example, let's say a problem begins with the number 96. You have to find ⅜ of this, then find the square root of the answer. Multiply that by 18, and find ⅝ of the result. Find 85 percent of that figure, and then multiply the result by 9 and subtract 375, divide the answer by 7, and then take ⅔ of the figure that results.

The final figure from this series of operations is 8, but try to do this in a limited time and without a calculator or pencil and paper, and you have a challenging mental arithmetic test.

The point of exercises like these is to make dealing with numbers an easy and routine task, leaving you free to shift your focus to the more complex assignments in which number-crunching is taken for granted.

Build numerical reasoning

Using math to solve real problems calls for more than the ability to add, divide, subtract, or multiply. Instead, you have to carry out numerical reasoning, to work out how to get the answer you want from the information you're given. Or you may be given data relating to a real life decision, and you have to interpret that data to make the best choice you can in that particular situation. In some cases, you may not even be dealing with precise figures at all—you might have to estimate, say, the amount of material you need for a particular task as quickly and accurately as you can.

Challenge yourself

Turning everyday situations in your life into math will help build your skills. For example, here's a real-life situation for

Alfred, Bill, and Charlie: The guys need 252 bottles of wine for a large holiday gathering. How many cases must they buy if there are 12 bottles to the case?

This is a simple division problem: 252 divided by 12 equals 21, therefore the solution is 21 cases.

Here's one that's a little more complicated: The three friends visit a wine auction and buy different quantities of wine. Alfred buys ⅖ of the total, Bill buys 20 percent of that total, and Charlie buys 24 bottles. So how many bottles did they buy in all?

The key is to work out what proportion of the total is made up of Charlie's 24 bottles. Since Alfred is buying ⅖ of the total (or 40 percent), and Bill is buying 20 percent, Charlie's 24 bottles represent the remaining 40 percent of the total. This means they bought 60 bottles in all.

Other examples look at how the ages of brothers and sisters in a family change as time passes. Let's say the ages of three children in your family added up to 19 two years ago—what will they add up to in two years' time? Start with the amount of time that has passed—between two years ago and two years in the future, four years will have passed. So each

child will be four years older. With three children, the total will increase by 12. This means in two years' time, their ages will add up to 19 plus 12, or 31.

Work out the rules

Most problems need a combination of numerical ability and logic to find the right approach for solving an individual problem. Other numerical problems approach logic problems even more closely by providing a series of numbers and asking what the next number in the sequence will be. This means working out the rules governing the progression between each term in the series and the next number. Once you work that out, all you have to do is apply the same rules to the final term in the question to determine your answer.

Some numerical problems follow the same rules as problems in other areas of brain testing. For example, filling in a crossword grid from a specific list of words is sometimes used as a numerical test, with the "words" represented by number combinations of varying lengths fitted into the correct spaces in the grid. In this case, the questions are usually simpler, with the choice of digits limited to 0 to 9 or 10 possibilities, rather than the 26 available options of a word-based puzzle. One square is usually completed to provide a starting point, and the technique for solving the rest means trying the next combinations on a trial-and-error basis until the whole puzzle can be completed with the correct number combinations. By the time you finish practicing this type of problem, your brain will be razor sharp!

Work the Puzzles

Many of the puzzles on the following pages are series problems, or sudokus,

Solving a sudoku each day will sharpen your brain.

which follow preset rules. In the case of sudokus, you have to use the rules given to find out where the numbers in each square, column, and row can be placed without breaking those rules. In the series problems you have to figure out the rule in each case before you can solve the problem. Keep an open mind—in one case, the numbers are equal to the letters that make up each word of the question!

For other puzzles, such as "Highway Robbery" (p. 107), take the numbers you don't know, such as the amount the robber took from each victim, and give each a symbol such as x and y. Then work out the relationship between x and y in the puzzle, and use the other information to work out the actual values of x and y themselves.

With most of these puzzles, look out for logic traps. If a store owner raises his prices by 10 percent and then lowers them by 10 percent, don't assume this brings them back to where they were before. If the price of something that costs $10 is cut by 10 percent, then the new price is $9 exactly. But if that price is raised by 10 percent, then the new price is $9.90, not $10!

> "Pure mathematics is, in its way, the poetry of logical ideas."
>
> —ALBERT EINSTEIN

Practice routines

How can exercising your mathematical ability improve your performance?

Most numerical puzzles use the basic arithmetical functions—addition, subtraction, multiplication, and division—and they need to become second nature so that your mind is freed up to take on more advanced tasks.

To get the exercise your brain needs, try drawing up columns of large numbers containing more and more digits, and add them up as quickly as possible. Or give yourself a series of subtraction sums using long, multidigit numbers, and try to perform the calculations as quickly as you can.

Some multiplication problems involve ratios and fractions as well as calculating the products of long numbers. Practicing all these helps improve mental agility.

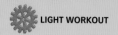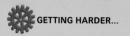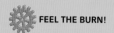
Numerical Puzzles

Math problems may seem challenging at first, but your skills will improve as you work your way through the levels of games. Your numerical reasoning is key; figure out the rules and you'll be able to find the answer every time. Don't be afraid to try the more difficult puzzles, and they'll soon be as quick and easy as a "light workout."

2 A Question of Division

How many of the numbers from 1 to 100 inclusive are divisible without remainder by either 2 or 3 or both?

1 Lighters

If you buy as many lighters as the number of cents each lighter costs, the total coming to $2.89, how many did you buy?

3 Getting Even

Which permutation of the nine digits 1 through 9 inclusive should you add to the number 123456789 to produce the largest possible answer consisting of even digits only?

Handy Hint

The total must be a 9-digit number if all the digits are to be even. (Why?) The highest 9-digit number with all even digits would be 888888888. But that is not possible. So how close can you get to it?

NEUROBIC TIP

4 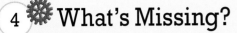 What's Missing?

Which 2-digit number is missing from this set?

61, 52, 63, 94, * 18

Handy Hint

This puzzle is more about spotting patterns than about the numbers 61, 52, 63... Try reversing the order of the digits in each "number."

NEUROBIC TIP

5 On Its Own Out Front

Which single digit should replace the question mark?

* 41, 12, 82, 53, 24, 94, 65

Handy Hint

Something has been done to the numbers to disguise the otherwise obvious pattern! But what?

NEUROBIC TIP

6 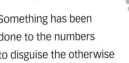 What Comes Next?

Which two-digit number comes next:

36, 91, 21, 51, 82, 12, 42 *

7 What Comes Next 2?

What comes next in this sequence:

3, 3, 5, 4, 4, 3, 5, 5, 4, 3 *

Handy Hint

Sometimes the puzzle is not in the numbers, but in the space between them.

NEUROBIC TIP

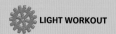

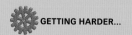

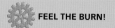

8 Look at the Question!

What should the next number be in the following sequence?

4, 6, 3, 4, 6, 2, 2, 3, 9 *

9 Calculating Weight

A meteorite weighs 1 pound plus ⅕ of its weight. How much does it weigh?

Handy Hint

NEUROBIC TIP

Think of the meteorite in one pan of a set of scales, with a pound weight and ⅕ of a meteorite of the same kind in the other pan.

10 Calculating Weight 2

A gold bar weighs ⅘ of an ingot plus ⅘ of a pound. How much does it weigh?

11 Same Difference

Subtract 2 and divide by 3 and you'll get the same answer as if you had added 4 and divided by 4. What answer is that? What is the starting number?

Think Positive

NEUROBIC TIP

Boost brain power in solving workplace problems by working in teams, using brainstorming sessions to churn out ideas as fast as possible. Most will be useless, but one may be just what you're looking for.

12 ❋ Highway Robbery

The highway robber Dick Terrapin, seeing that Mr. Rich had 100 gold pieces and that Ms. Loaded had 200, took 3 times as much from Ms. Loaded as he did from Mr. Rich. As a result, Mr. Rich ended up with twice as much as Ms. Loaded. How much did Dick Terrapin ride off with?

13 ❋ Price Shuffle

A storekeeper raised his prices one week by 10 percent, then a week later reduced them by 10 percent. Are prices back to where they were before the price shuffle?

Don't Make Assumptions

Where a problem involves two unknown but related factors, try to work out the relationship between them. If an object weighs a given amount plus a fraction of its total weight, then the weight given represents the remainder of the total. For example, an elephant weighs 3 tons plus ¼ of its weight. That means 3 tons is the other ¾ of the elephant's total weight. It must weigh 4 tons. But watch out for questions about raising or lowering prices—cutting prices by a percentage, then raising them by the same percentage doesn't bring you back to the numbers you started with because you are starting from a different baseline.

14 ❋ A Missed Opportunity

A shopkeeper lowered his prices one week by a certain percentage only to raise them again by the exact same percentage. As a result, a grommet that had cost $1 before the price changes, now costs 36 cents. If only I had bought one after the first price change, how much would it have cost?

15 ⚙ The Dog-Eared Packs

Karen's dog, Rover, chewed up some of her playing cards. Dealing the remaining cards out 2 at a time left Karen with 1 extra card, 3 at a time left 2 extra, 4 at a time left 3 extra, and 5 at a time left 4. How many cards of the original two packs were left?

Handy Hint

We are looking for a number that leaves a remainder of 1 when we divide by 2; a remainder of 2 when we divide by 3; a remainder of 3 when we divide by 4; and a remainder of 4 when we divide by 5. There are 52 cards in a pack.

16 ⚙ Express Train

How long does it take an express train a mile long to go completely through a tunnel a mile long at a mile per minute?

Handy Hint

Don't forget the train has to go in and it has to come out!

17 ⚙ Like Clockwork

Buses arrive like clockwork in Bustown. That's because the mayor has decreed that they maintain a steady speed of exactly 50 miles per hour at all times. On one such bus, leaving by the only road leading in and out of town, you notice that you meet a bus coming the other way every 3 minutes. How many buses arrive at Bustown each hour?

18 Seven Pluses

By inserting exactly 7 plus signs in the left-hand string of numbers, make this sum true.

1234567890 = 180

Handy Hint

You could have 1-digit numbers, 2-digit numbers, and 3-digit numbers. Think how many of each kind you need.

19 Getting By

The sum below is correct. Now rewrite it without changing the order of the digits but managing with one fewer plus sign on the left: $1 + 2 + 3 + 4 + 56 + 7 + 8 + 9 = 90$

21 A Reversal

If you multiply 4321 by a certain 4-digit number, the 8-digit answer you get ends in its reverse, such as 1234. That's to say: $4321 \times **** = ****1234$

What is the 4-digit number?

20 The Squeeze

A wet sponge weighs 1 kilogram and is 99 percent water by weight. Squeeze it so it is only 98 percent water by weight. How much does it weigh now?

Keep on Breathing...

All these questions call for a clear head, and clear, unhurried thinking. Studies show that breathing slowly and deeply increases oxygen intake and boosts blood flow to the brain, with definite improvements in performance.

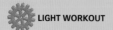

22 Number Stack 1

The number in each box has to equal the sum of the numbers in the two boxes immediately under it, except in the bottom row, which has no boxes under it. The numbers in some of the boxes have already been filled in. How quickly can you fill in the others?

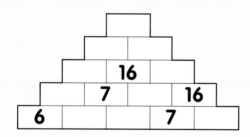

23 Number Stack 2

The number in each of these boxes has to be the sum of the numbers in the two boxes immediately under it. Except, that is, for the bottom row, the boxes of which have no other boxes beneath them. No two boxes can have the same number in them. Can you fill in the missing numbers?

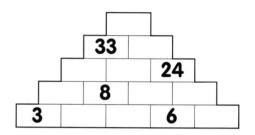

24 Number Stack 3

The number in each of these boxes is to be the sum of the numbers in the two boxes immediately under it. Except, that is, for the bottom row, which has no other boxes beneath them. Can you fill in the missing numbers in such a way as to minimize the number in the top box? Whole numbers greater than zero only, please! No number may be repeated in the construction of the number stack!

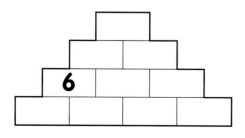

25 Squares

How many different squares can you find in the following grid?

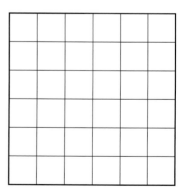

26 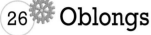 Oblongs

How many different oblongs can you find in the grid shown? (An oblong is a rectangle that isn't a square!)

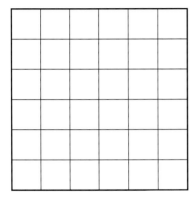

27 ABRACADABRA!

How many ways are there of spelling ABRACADABRA if you start at the top and proceed downward one level at a time and you are only allowed to travel to adjacent letters?

```
            A
           B B
          R R R
         A A A A
        C C C C C
       A A A A A A
      D D D D D D D
     A A A A A A A A
    B B B B B B B B B
   R R R R R R R R R R
  A A A A A A A A A A A
```

28 Game Show

In a futuristic game show, you have to choose a single letter from each level of the board starting with the top letter and working your way down, level by level. How many ways are there to spell TRIANGLE, starting at the T at the top and going down a level at a time? You need to choose the first letter from the first row, the second from somewhere in the second row, the third letter from somewhere in the third row, and so on right down to the bottom row from which the E at the end of TRIANGLE must be chosen.

```
         T
        R R
       I I I
      A A A A
     N N N N N
    G G G G G G
   L L L L L L L
  E E E E E E E E
```

29 In Addition

Write the number 54 using each of the digits 1, 6, 8, and 9 once, and once only. In addition—if you'll pardon the pun—you may use: parentheses ( ), plus signs +, minus signs –, multiplication signs x, and division signs / ! This is a near miss:

(6 x 8) + 9 – 1

30 Coconuts

A castaway was stuck on a desert island with only coconuts to eat. Thank goodness he also had a decent supply of fresh water. As for the coconuts, he divided them into 7 equal heaps with no coconuts left over. If he had divided them into 6, 5, 4, 3, or 2 heaps, there would have been 1 left over in every case. What is the fewest coconuts he could have had?

Handy Hint

Puzzle 15 is a good warm-up for Puzzle 30.

31 Choose Your Mates

Tricky Teach, the pirate, had to choose 4 out of 8 men to come ashore and 4 to watch the boat. Now 4 of these 8 were his friends and 4 his sworn enemies. To give the appearance of fairness, he always chose his men by putting them in a circle on the poop deck and counting off every fifth man counterclockwise starting from the man nearest the stern until 4 were chosen. Once a man was counted out, he left the circle and Teach continued counting those remaining. So it was vital that Teach put his 4 pals in the right places in the circle, which he did. But he changed his mind and decided he wanted to stay onboard and it was his enemies he wanted to send ashore. The men were already in their places, and the tradition was to count from the stern-most man counterclockwise, so the only remedy was to not choose every fifth man—but every how many?

Handy Hint

Sketch 8 men (dots!) in a circle. Starting with the man nearest the stern, work out which men would be picked out if you discard every fifth, counting counterclockwise.

32 Pyramids

The cannonballs in Napoleon's camp in his Egyptian barracks are arranged in pyramid shapes. Each layer in such a pyramid is a square of cannonballs having one fewer along its edge than the layer immediately under it (except, of course, for the bottom layer, which rests on the ground!). You count 14 layers in one such pyramid. Is the number of balls in the stack odd? Or even? What about another pyramid of cannonballs containing 11 layers?

33 What Comes Next 3?

What digit may be inserted between the 1 and 5 on the top of the fraction $\frac{15}{51}$ and the 5 and 1 on the bottom in order that the fraction stay the same in value?

Mind Your Language

For a long-term brain exercise, try learning to speak a new language. This stretches the brain in every kind of way, and you can go on improving your abilities over a lifetime.

NEUROBIC TIP

34 Rice Pudding

Here are 3 different offers for rice pudding at the supermarket. Which is the best value for the money? Why might you buy the most expensive?

50%
Extra!

Buy one
get one
free!

40%
off!

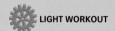

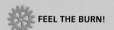
35 A Simple Calculation

Divide the face of this calculator into a number of pieces so that the numbers on each piece add up to the same total.

7	8	9
4	5	6
1	2	3
0		

Handy Hint

What is the sum of the digits?

36 A Tricky Number

Divide the face of this telephone into a number of pieces so that the numbers in each piece add up to the same *even* number. Cut along the lines only!

1	2	3
4	5	6
7	8	9
	0	

37 Round the Clock 1

Divide the clock face shown into two sections so that the numbers on each segment add up to the same number.

Handy Hint

What is the total of all the numbers on the clock face?

38 Round the Clock 2

Divide the clock face shown into three sections so that the numbers on each segment add up to the same number.

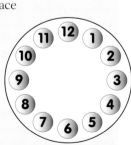

39 ✸ Sudoku 1

Fill in the grid in such a way that each and every row, column, and 3 x 3 box contains all the numbers from 1 to 9. You don't need outstanding math skills, just logic and reasoning.

1					5		6	
		7		4				1
4				7	6			
	2				4		3	5
		4		1		2		6
8		6	2	5			9	
6			4				1	
		8			3			
	4						7	9

 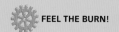
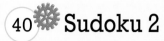

40 Sudoku 2

Fill in the grid in such a way that each and every row, column, and 3 x 3 box contains all the numbers from 1 to 9. You don't need outstanding math skills, just logic and reasoning.

1						8	9	
7			1			4		
4	8	9			6			
		4	3	9		7		
		7	6	2	1			
3			8		7		5	2
		1		6				
6	3	2			8	9		
		8			2			

41 ✿ Sudoku 3

Fill in the grid in such a way that each and every row, column, and 3 x 3 box contains all the numbers from 1 to 9. You don't need outstanding math skills, just logic and reasoning.

				9			5	1
4					3			7
1		9			2			
	3	6						
2			9					6
	9		7				3	
	2		4			5		8
7	8		3					
9						4		

42 Sudoku 4

Fill in the grid in such a way that each and every row, column, and 3 x 3 box contains all the numbers from 1 to 9. You don't need outstanding maths skills, just logic and reasoning.

	4	6					2	9
			9	3				
		1					4	
				5	9			
5	2							
			8	2			3	
			7		1			
				3			8	6
1					2			5

43 Sudoku 5

Fill in the grid in such a way that each and every row, column, and 3 x 3 box contains all the numbers from 1 to 9. You don't need outstanding math skills, just logic and reasoning.

	3							
		4		6		9	2	7
6	2		4		9		5	
8		6				5	9	
	7		1	9	6		4	2
4	9		8	3	5	1	7	
9		1	2					8
7		8	6		3	2	1	9
			9	1	8	7	6	

1. $289 = 1 \times 289$, 17×17, or 289×1. That means we have either one lighter costing \$2.89, or 289 lighters each costing 1cent. Neither of these is particularly likely. So we go for 17 lighters at 17 cents each. Note that after all the numerical work has been done, you should check up on the reasonableness of the answer.

2. The number of numbers in the range 1 to 100 exactly divisible by 2, which is $100/2 = 50$. The number divisible by 3 is $99/3 = 33$. The number divisible by both is the number divisible by 6, namely $96/6 = 16$. By adding $50 + 33$, we are including twice those numbers that are divisible by 2 and divisible by 3, i.e., by 6. To remove this over-counting, we need to subtract 16, so the answer is $50 + 33 - 16 = 67$.

3. 765429831. Added to 123456789 this gives 888886620.

4. Reversing the order of the digits, we get: 16, 25, 36, 49 * 81. We recognize the two-digit squares: $4 \times 4 = 16$; $5 \times 5 = 25$; $6 \times 6 = 36$; $7 \times 7 = 49$. The next square is $8 \times 8 = 64$. Reversing this gives 46.

5. These are the successive multiples of 7 with the order of the digits reversed: 7, 14, 21, 28, 35, 42, 49, 56... which becomes 7, 41, 12, 82, 53, 24, 94, 65... once the order of the digits is reversed. 7 is a 1-digit number so it remains the same when its order is reversed.

6. The successive multiples of 3 are: 3, 6, 9, 12, 15, 18, 21, 24, 27, 30 ... Regrouping these in pairs gives 36, 91, 21, 51, 82, 12, 42, 73 ... So the next element in the sequence is 73.

7. This is not so much a puzzle about numbers as about the number of letters in a spelled-out number. The next number in the sequence is 6. These are the numbers of letters in the spelled numbers: ONE, TWO, THREE, FOUR, and so on. There are 6 letters in ELEVEN.

8. These are the numbers of letters in successive words of the question. There are 8 letters in SEQUENCE.

9. Four-fifths of the meteorite must weigh a pound. So ⅕ must weigh a quarter of a pound, or 0.25 lb. The whole must weigh 1.25 pounds.

10. Multiply everything by 5. Five ingots must weigh the same as 4 ingots and 4 pounds. So 1 ingot must weigh 4 pounds.

11. Twenty is the starting number and 6 is the number you end up with.

12. This can be solved by trial and error. However, an algebraic result is more certain. Let the amount Terrapin takes from Rich be x. Then he takes $3x$ from Ms. Loaded. So we know that $100 - x = 2(200 - 3x)$. The right-hand side equals $400 - 6x$. That means $300 - 5x$, so that $x = 60$. Checking, Terrapin takes 60 from Rich, leaving him with 40. He must take 3 times as much from Ms. Loaded, which is 180. This leaves her with $200 - 180 = 20$. That is all fine, since 40 is twice 20, as required. Terrapin went off with $4x = 240$ gold pieces.

13. No, things aren't back to how they were. Imagine something that costs \$1. After a 10 percent increase this becomes \$1.10.

After the 10 percent decrease this becomes 99 cents. So prices are lower than before the price shuffle.

14. The grommet would have cost 20 cents. This can be solved by trial and error. The first step is to find the percentage drop. If we lower the price by 50 percent and raise it by 50 percent, something costing a dollar will at the halfway point cost 50 cents, then at the end will cost 75 cents. So we are looking for a percentage decrease of more than 50 percent. You should be able to hit upon 80 percent.

   To solve this systematically, call the price reduction x percent. Then after the first price change, things will cost a fraction $((100 - x)/100)$ of what they did before. After the price hike, they will cost a fraction $((100 - x)/100)$ of what they did just before the price hike. The net result is that they cost $(100 - x)/100 \times (100 + x)/100$ of what they did before. That is, $(10{,}000 - x^2)/10{,}000) \times 100$ cents = 36 cents. That is $10{,}000 - x^2 = 3600$, $x^2 = 6400$, which means $x = 80$. So he reduced prices by 80 percent and then raised them by 80 percent. If I had bought a grommet after the first price change, it would have cost me 20 cents.

15. If you had one more card, there would be no remainder from division by 2, 3, 4, and 5. The smallest number divisible by 2, 3, 4, and 5 is the smallest number divisible by 3, 4, and 5. This is 60. So the required number is 1 less: 59. Check that it leaves the required remainders after division.

16. The train has to travel a mile to fully enter the tunnel and then

another mile for the back of the train to clear the tunnel. So we need to know how long it takes to go 2 miles at 1 mile a minute—which is 2 minutes.

17. If your bus stopped, the rate at which buses pass you would halve. So then you would be passed by a bus every 6 minutes. So 10 buses per hour arrive at Bustown.

18. $1 + 2 + 3 + 4 + 5 + 67 + 8 + 90 = 180$ uses 7 plus signs. This can be reached by intelligently guided trial and error. If we want the sum to be a 3-digit number, we need all the rest to be 1-digit numbers to give us the opportunity of using 7 plus signs. The 3-digit number can only be 123 as this is the only one possible that is less than 180. Unfortunately, $123 + 4 + 5 + 6 + 7 + 8 + 9 + 0$ does not equal 180. So we do not want a 3-digit number. It follows that we want a pair of two-digit numbers and 6 single-digit numbers. We want the two 2-digit numbers to be about half 180. If we do *not* choose 90 as one of them, then the most we can make is $1 + 2 + 3 + 4 + 5 + 67 + 89 + 0$, which is short of 180. So it follows we must use the 90. $1 + 2 + 3 + 4 + 5 + 6 + 78 + 90$ overshoots, so we stumble on $1 + 2 + 3 + 5 + 67 + 8 + 90$ which works exactly.

Alternatively, we can adopt an algebraic approach. Inserting signs promotes some of the digits to the tens place. Let the sum of the digits in the tens places equal x, and those left in the ones places equal y. $10x + y = 180$. But $x + y = 45$ (the sum of the digits). So we see that $9x = 180 - 45 = 135$. This means $x = 15$. We want the sum of the numbers in the tens places to equal 15. We want a pair of 2-digit

numbers. It can't be $7 + 8$ as these are adjacent in the list so they can't both be the first digit of a 2-digit number. This leaves only $6 + 9$, leading at once to $1 + 2 + 3 + 4 + 5 + 67 + 8 + 90$.

19. Here we have 5 in the tens place. If we can somehow manufacture a situation in which we have a total of 5 in the tens places, the units are bound to come to the same total as before. Do you see why? $5 = 1 + 4$, or $2 + 3$. We cannot promote both 2 and 3 to tens places as they are adjacent in the string of digits. So we need to promote 1 and 4, giving: $12 + 3 + 45 + 6 + 7 + 8 + 9 = 90$.

20. Half a kilogram. Originally 1 percent of the weight is sponge (10 grams out of 1000 grams). Finally 2 percent of the weight is sponge. 10 grams out of half as much: i.e. 500 grams!)

21. $4321 \times 9954 = 43011234$. [Start with $4321 \times *c*a = ****1234$. Clearly $a = 4$. Then try $4321 \times **b4 = ****1234$. The tens digit in the answer must come from $(2 \times 4) + (1 \times b)$. That is, from $8 + b$. If $8 + b$ is to end in 3, b must be 5. Now try $4321 \times *c54 = ****1234$. Proceeding step-by-step with the 100s and 1000s digits, we soon come up with 9954 as the multiplier. The rest follows.

22. It is fairly simple to deduce the ringed numbers. Once these are known, it is straightforward to fill in the rest.

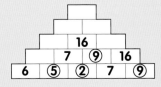

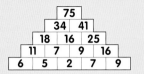

23. Let us label the two numbers under 8 with an a and b. Clearly $a + b = 8$.

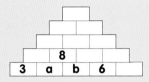

Of the various possiblities, only $1+7$ or $7+1$ involve numbers not used twice.

If we let $a=1$ and $b=7$, we end up with 7 in the second row above the 1 and 6. So the only possibility is that $a =1$ and $b=7$. The stack then has the appearance shown below.

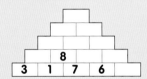

It is then relatively easy to fill in the remaining boxes.

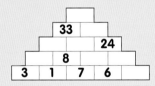

This leads to:

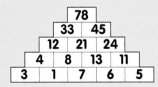

24. Start by filling in the bottom row with letters representing the unknown numbers.

(Continued on page 122)

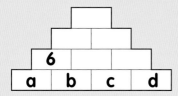

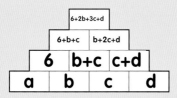

It is then possible to fill in each square by adding together the two squares on which it rests.

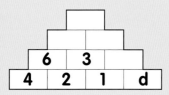

The topmost square contains $6 + 2b + 3c + d$. Clearly we need to minimize c to make 3c as small as possible, so we can let $c = 1$. Next, we want to minimize b, but we may not use 1 as that has already been used, so we let $b = 2$. We then have the solution shown.

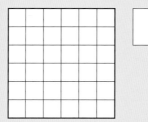

We want the next available free number for d. 1–4 have been used. We can't use 5 or we get a second 6 above the 1 and the d. The next free number is, in fact, 7. Filling in with $d = 7$ leads to the solution shown.

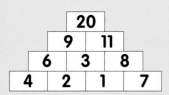

25. 91 in all. There are 6 x 6 = 36 squares of size 1 x 1. Now let's consider how many squares there that are of the size 2 x 2. Imagine a 2 x 2 tile that has to be aligned with the lines of the grid. There are 5 positions horizontally and 5 positions vertically. This makes 5 x 5 positions in all.

Repeating the same trick with a 3 x 3 tile we find that there are 4 x 4 of these. There are therefore: 36 + 25 + 16 + 9 + 4 + 1 = 91 squares in all.

26. Any allowable rectangle can be specified by choosing a pair of vertical lines and a pair of horizontal lines.

Specifying a rectangle

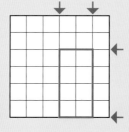

There are 7 ways of choosing the first of the vertical lines and 6 ways of choosing the second line. So at first sight, you might think there are therefore 7 x 6 = 42 ways of choosing a pair of vertical lines. But we have counted each pair twice, since we could equally well have chosen the first line second and the second line first, although

this would have been exactly the same pair of lines. So the number of ways of choosing a vertical pair of lines is 7 x 6/2 = 21. The same applies for the horizontal pair of lines. We will combine these to make a rectangle. So there are 21 x 21 = 441 rectangles. Since 91 of these rectangles are actually squares, we must have 441 – 91 = 350 oblongs.

27. At each transition you have two choices: You can turn leftish or turn rightish. There are 11 letters in ABRACADABRA and so 10 transitions. So there are 2 x 2 x 2 x 2 x 2 x 2 x 2 x 2 x 2 x 2 = 2^{10} = 1024.

Allowed transitions

28. Nearly 40 million ways. (There is 1 way of choosing the first letter. This can be combined with 2 ways of choosing the second letter, which may be combined with 3 ways of choosing the third letter, and so on. . . . This gives 1 x 2 x 3 x 4 x 5 x 6 x 7 x 8 x 9 x 10 x 11 = 39,916,800.)

29. 6/ (1 – 8/9). Is there any other way?

30. If he set aside the single troublesome coconut that is always left over, he would be able to divide them by 6, 5, 4, 3, and 2. The smallest number divisible by 6, 4, 3, and 2 is 12. The smallest number divisible by 12 and 5 is 60. Any multiple of 60 will automatically be divisible by 6, 5, 4, 3, and 2. So the number of

coconuts he has is a multiple of 60 plus the 1 coconut he set aside. So he must have the smallest number in this sequence which is also divisible by 7:

61, 121, 181, 241, 301, 361...

By trial and error we find this to be 301.

31. If you count out every fifth man counterclockwise, you knock out the men you don't want. To pick the others, you need instead to count every ninth man.

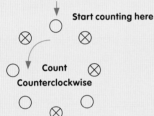

Start counting here

Count Counterclockwise

32. The numbers in each layer starting from the top go as follows: 1, 4, 9, 16, 25... That is, odd, even, odd, even... With a pyramid of 14 layers, we have 7 odd layers and 7 evens. This comes to an odd number. With 11 layers, we have 6 odd layers (giving an even number in total) and 5 even layers. So such a pyramid of 11 square layers contains an even number of cannonballs.

33. $\frac{15}{51} = \frac{165}{561}$ As there are only 10 digits we could simply check

$\frac{115}{511}, \frac{125}{521}, \frac{135}{531} \ldots \frac{185}{581}, \frac{195}{591},$

to see which, if any, equals More logically we can let: $\frac{15}{51}$.

$\frac{1A5}{5A1} = \frac{15}{51}$ and try to find the value of the digit A.
$51 \times (1A5) = 5A1 \times 15$
but $1A5 = 105 + 10A$
and $5A1 = 501 + 10A$. So:

$51 \times (105 + 10A) = 15 \times (501 + 10A)$.
$51 \times 105 + 510A = 15 \times 501 + 150A$
$5335 + 510A = 7515 + 150A$
$360A = 2160$. $36A = 216$;
so $A = 6$.

34. It can't be the first offer, since you only get 1½ cans for your money, whereas for the second you get 2 cans for your money. The third offer says you pay only 60 cents in the dollar for the can. So you could get 1⅔ of a can for the same money. So the second offer is the best value for money, the third is second best, and the first is the worst!

35. The total of the digits is 45. The largest number is 9, so whatever the total on each piece, it must be at least 9. But it can't be 9, or what would go with the 7? It's too far from the 2! So the total should be 15, and we need 3 pieces. This can be simply achieved as shown.

7	8	9
4	5	6
1	2	3
0		

36. There is no point in inverting the piece with the 6 and 9 as that just gives you a 9 and a 6—with the same total (see diagram a below). But you could invert the 8 and the 9. This gives a 6 and an 8 (and a 0) which comes to 14 (see b) It is then a simple matter to divide the remaining part of the keypad to give two lots of 14 (see diagram c)

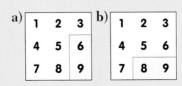

a)
1	2	3
4	5	6
7	8	9

b)
1	2	3
4	5	6
7	8	9

c)
1	2	3
4	5	6
7	8	9

37. The total of the numbers on the clock face is 78. So each part must have numbers that total half of this, namely, 39. This is how it can be done (see digaram a).

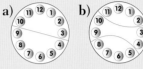

a) b)

38. The total of the numbers on the clock is 78. So each section must carry a total of 78/3 = 26. This is how it can be done (see diagram b).

39.

1	8	2	9	3	5	4	6	7
3	6	7	8	4	2	9	5	1
4	9	5	1	7	6	3	2	8
9	2	1	6	8	4	7	3	5
7	5	4	3	1	9	2	8	6
8	3	6	2	5	7	1	9	4
6	7	9	4	2	8	5	1	3
5	1	8	7	9	3	6	4	2
2	4	3	5	6	1	8	7	9

40.

1	2	3	5	7	4	8	9	6
7	6	5	1	8	9	4	2	3
4	8	9	2	3	6	5	1	7
2	1	4	3	9	5	7	6	8
8	5	7	6	2	1	3	4	9
3	9	6	8	4	7	1	5	2
5	7	1	9	6	3	2	8	4
6	3	2	4	1	8	9	7	5
9	4	8	7	5	2	6	3	1

41.

3	7	2	8	9	4	6	5	1
4	5	8	1	6	3	9	2	7
1	6	9	5	7	2	3	8	4
5	3	6	2	8	1	7	4	9
2	4	7	9	3	5	8	1	6
8	9	1	7	4	6	2	3	5
6	2	3	4	1	7	5	9	8
7	8	4	3	5	9	1	6	2
9	1	5	6	2	8	4	7	3

42.

3	4	6	5	1	8	7	2	9
2	7	8	9	4	3	6	5	1
9	5	1	2	7	6	8	4	3
8	3	4	1	5	9	2	6	7
5	2	7	3	6	4	9	1	8
6	1	9	8	2	7	5	3	4
4	6	5	7	8	1	3	9	2
7	9	2	4	3	5	1	8	6
1	8	3	6	9	2	4	7	5

43.

1	3	9	5	7	2	6	8	4
5	8	4	3	6	1	9	2	7
6	2	7	4	8	9	3	5	1
8	1	6	7	2	4	5	9	3
3	7	5	1	9	6	8	4	2
4	9	2	8	3	5	1	7	6
9	6	1	2	5	7	4	3	8
7	5	8	6	4	3	2	1	9
2	4	3	9	1	8	7	6	5

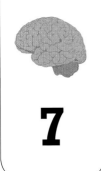

7

Hold That Thought!

Improving your memory is as easy as a walk in the park—a blessing, since memory is essential for a sharp brain that knows where you left your keys and what time you're supposed to meet a friend.

There are two types of memory: working memory and long-term memory. Working memory, which is used to absorb new information, holds that information for as long as necessary, much like the random access memory (RAM) of a computer. Keep the computer on and the memory is there. Shut it down and it's gone. Research has shown that between 80 and 90 percent of information stored in working memory during the course of a day is forgotten by bedtime. At some point during the day, your brain decides you no longer need it and dumps it in your cranial trash can. Adding to the problem is the fact that working memory can store only around seven or eight items of information at any moment. Most of us can usually remember a seven-digit telephone number, for example, but we struggle to recall a longer series of letters, symbols, or numbers.

Boosting Your Memory

Can anything be done to boost working-memory capacity?

As with so many other aspects of brain fitness, practice helps up to a point. After a while, the brain becomes more accustomed to storing and retaining larger items of data at a time. But a study by two psychology professors at Syracuse University showed that even that improvement is still relatively small. They gave five adult volunteers a series of 10 one-hour tests spread over five days, in which they were shown numbers for a two-second period on a computer monitor.

After seeing a series of numbers, the volunteers were then shown a second series and asked if there were any differences from the numbers in the first series. As each series became longer and more complex, performance suffered but,

in time, the volunteers were able to deal with four columns of numbers at once, though stretching that to five still caused performance to suffer.

Play games that challenge the mind

While it can be difficult to boost memory with certain conventional activities, research at Stirling University in Scotland using young adolescents suggests there may be indirect ways of boosting working-memory performance. It was found that playing video games that involve elements of planning and strategy and playing sudoku (logical and spatial number puzzles) both improved memory.

Stay in touch

The Stirling University study also found that social tasks, such as keeping in touch with friends on Facebook rather than absorbing predigested information on

Playing video games that involve elements of planning and strategy and playing sudoku (logical and spatial number puzzles) helps improve memory.

Twitter, produced a measurable increase in the amount of information their subjects could store in working memory. Beginning to realize why your kids can remember more than you do?

Build a Better Memory

Just as a computer operator will save important information for long-term storage on the machine's hard drive until it's needed or updated, retaining information in the brain depends on moving it from working memory to long-term memory, then saving it.

That can be tough. In the nineteenth century, German psychologist Herman Ebbinghaus studied how we remember what we've learned. He set out to learn a list of 20 meaningless syllables such as BOJ, LUB, TUR, and WUT, from a choice of 2,000. When he had learned a full list of 20 syllables, he tried repeating the list at longer intervals to see how well the information was retained. He found 75 percent was forgotten within two weeks and almost 80 percent in a month. He also found that the syllables at the start and end of the list were retained longer, but words printed in contrasting colors were remembered the best of all.

These studies helped show how we learn, and later research with groups of students revealed even more. Some students practiced memory tests over and over, others learned specific techniques for improving the memorizing process, and still others did neither of these tasks.

Surprisingly, the results showed that practicing memorization had no effect at all in comparison with students who made no conscious effort to improve performance. Only those individuals who learned and practiced specific techniques for implanting information in long-term memory improved their performance significantly. Here are some of the best.

Picture a fish riding a bicycle

One technique for improving your memory is to put the items into a pattern—a story, for example. When the names themselves don't fit the story easily, choose words that are close enough to aid recall and try to imagine pictures of the actions you are describing.

Experience shows that the more absurd these pictures are, the easier it is to remember them: A fish riding a bicycle will stand out more clearly in your memory than an everyday, logical image of someone driving a car or boarding a bus.

The reason this technique works is that it fits the separate items on the list into a pattern, and our brains are constantly trying to spot patterns in everyday chaos. But the same story will not work for two lists. So if you are faced with a different list of things to remember, try forming a completely different pattern.

Tour the house

Another regularly used method is to imagine each object in a different place in your house, then picture yourself walking around, through doors and up and down stairs, to identify each against its background as a clear mental picture.

Visualize a walk to work

A third idea is to link the objects you'd like to remember to different places on your journey to or from work, again visualizing the mental pictures to fix each item in its correct location.

Play word association games

Word associations also help. Anyone having trouble remembering whether to adjust clocks backward or forward when switching to and from Daylight Savings Time can use the formula "Spring forward, fall back." Others find it helpful to link a complex piece of information to a popular tune, so singing the information helps to bridge any gaps.

For the same reason, Shakespeare's blank verse with its natural rhythms is usually easier to remember than prose of a similar length.

Mnemonics also help recall the order of things, such as the colors of the spectrum. Memorizing the name Roy G. Biv provides a reminder of the order of the colors of the rainbow—red, orange, yellow, green, blue, indigo, and violet. Or the notes of the treble staff of musical notation—E, G, B, D, F—produce the mnemonic "Every Good Boy Deserves Fudge."

Practice memory games

All these techniques help to improve our ability to transfer and store information in our long-term memory. Practicing them will produce marked improvements in the way we remember objects, facts, and figures. On a walk in the country or in the park, for example, try remembering all the objects you saw of a particular color in terms of what they were and where they were.

It won't take long to learn how to recall them in order by playing back the walk in your mind afterward.

"Memory: a child walking along a seashore. You never can tell what small pebble it will pick up and store away among its treasured things."

—PIERCE HARRIS

Between 80 and 90 percent of the information stored in working memory during the course of a day is actually forgotten by bedtime.

Work the Puzzles

Memory puzzles are unlike most other puzzles in this book.

Instead of puzzles that ask you to work from the information given to produce an answer that may be right or wrong, most of the puzzles in this section are exercises that help improve memory storage and retrieval—such as learning how rhythm and rhyme can help in learning verses from a poem. Or how they can sometimes be used as a way of remembering complex information. Or how joining a quiz team or trying to outdo competitors on TV quiz shows, by answering questions before they do, can boost memory as well.

Other exercises follow the basic principles of Kim's Game, first created by the writer Rudyard Kipling. The original involved placing a series of unrelated objects on a tray, hidden under a cloth. The cloth is removed and you're given a limited amount of time to memorize the objects before the cloth is replaced. Then, after a fixed time, you have to recall as many of the objects as you can.

Memory Can Change Your Brain

Neuroscientific research at Brown University has suggested that the processes of learning and committing information into long-term memory actually causes physical changes in the brain's internal wiring. A mechanism called long-term potentiation (LTP) makes it easier for interconnected brain cells involved in these processes to communicate efficiently with one another. Amazingly, these improved connections can last for weeks after the activity that brought them into being has stopped.

Still other memory exercises use faces, both famous and unknown, and childhood pictures of celebrities to match to the identities we now find familiar.

And finally, some of the puzzles ask you to compare different versions of the same picture with a few unobtrusive details altered. How many can you spot?

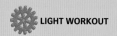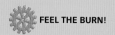
Memory Puzzles

Memory is very fluid and easy to improve. Your brain will respond to so many different stimuli that memory games have the fastest impact on overall performance. Try these puzzles for a range of challenges to boost your memory power, and use the exercises to get into good memory-enhancing habits.

1 Rhyme & Song

Rhyme and song naturally help us to remember because they link the purely verbal to other modalities of thinking. The more modalities that are engaged when we encounter a fact, the more memorable it becomes. To cultivate a sense of rhythm and rhyme, practice memorizing one poem daily. Choose one that appeals to you or that embodies something to which you can relate.

Start with a short one—such as a haiku—then proceed to quatrains, limericks, and sonnets. Rhyme helps to measure out the elements to be memorized, so choose verses that rhyme and that have some meaning for you. Repetition is helpful. Here are a couple to get you started:

I never saw a Purple Cow:
I never hope to see one;
But I can tell you, anyhow,
I'd rather see than be One.
        —*Gelett Burgess*

And:

To See a World in a Grain of Sand
And a Heaven in a Wild Flower
Hold Infinity in the palm of your hand
And Eternity in an hour.
        —*William Blake*

Which of these is easier to remember?

Why do you think this is?

Remember, it is easier to memorize if you break the poem down into sections, proceeding one chunk at a time. Repetition helps!

2 ✹ Verbal Practice

Cultivate the habit of listening to the lyrics of songs, and sing along with the radio or songs on a CD. If you are the shy type it might be better to cultivate this habit in private. Singing along with the radio or CD player encourages you to focus on the music, the words, and the intonation of the singer and makes lyrics more memorable. It is a great exercise, and children do this naturally when listening to pop music, but easily embarrassed adults lose this habit. A further step is to watch and imitate the video.

3 ✹ Out Shopping

There is much that can be done in everyday life to exercise one's memory. For example, when shopping, write your grocery list as usual. Look it over once, and put it in your back pocket or purse. Then go to the store. Just before reaching the checkout, go over the list to see if you have forgotten anything. Monitor your progress and see if you can do better next time.

You can also practice your calculating skills by estimating how much you have spent before the cashier rings it up. Can you work out the change before the cash register does?

Rosemary for Remembrance?

The key to improving overall brain performance depends on memory, and the herb rosemary has been linked to memory for centuries. Recent research suggests there may be some truth in its allegedly beneficial effects on the brain. Its active ingredient, carnosic acid, seems to provide protection from the damage caused by strokes and free radicals, but its effect is only triggered after the damage is inflicted.

NEUROBIC TIP

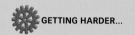
4 Joining a Quiz Team

One way of helping memory is to practice information retrieval. A social way of practicing this is by joining a group that plays Trivial Pursuit or other general knowledge games. This is fun and it also stimulates curiosity and the brain's retrieval powers. There are also many quiz programs on radio and TV, such as *Jeopardy* (for general knowledge) and *Who Wants to Be a Millionaire* (for variability in the difficulty of questions). Actively try to answer the questions ahead of the contestants. When you get questions wrong, check them on the Internet or in an encyclopedia and verify the answer.

Curiosity is the driving force behind inquiry. It is easiest to remember what intrigues you. Knowledge is a framework, and the more you know that is interesting and easy to remember, the easier it will be to remember the less fascinating facts. Read this list of fascinating facts, then close the book and see how many you can remember.

a) Mozart was age five when he composed his variations on "Twinkle, Twinkle Little Star."

b) The word "the" is the most commonly used word in the English language.

c) Gorillas can't swim.

d) A fly's tastebuds are in its feet.

e) The can opener was invented 48 years after cans were introduced.

f) There are no pain receptors in the brain, so the brain can feel no pain.

g) Admiral Nelson suffered from sea sickness.

h) The word "typewriter" is one of the longest words that can be written using only letters in the top row of a keyboard.

i) There are no octopuses in Arctic waters.

j) A rare breed of Double-Nosed Andean Tiger Hound, which has two noses, was discovered on a recent trip to Bolivia.

k) It was a Canadian journalist, Sandy Gardiner, who coined the term "Beatlemania."

5 List the Stories

After listening to the news, attempt to list the stories in order. Start with short newscasts like those on public radio stations or on-the-hour summaries on all-news stations, and then proceed to longer bulletins. It is also a useful trick to review in your mind what you have done each day and what remains to be done. It is a useful monitor of progress and helps you focus on your goals.

6 Misspellings

Here is a list of 20 words that are frequently misspelled. Look at them and try to devise a way of remembering how they should be spelled.

existence	buoyant
accommodate	daiquiri
harass	embarrass
camouflage	exaggerate
guerrilla	fluorescent
inoculate	gauge
withhold	hygiene
sacrilege	independent
separate	miniature
necessary	millennium

Now turn over the page and try to decide which, if any, of the words in the corresponding list, have been misspelled.

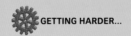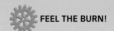

accomodate	harrass
bouyant	hygene
camouflage	independant
daquiri	innoculate
guerrilla	milennium
embarass	minature
exagerrate	necessary
existance	sacrelege
flourescent	seperate
guage	withold

7 Pronunciation

There are many ways of pronouncing the group of letters "ough." Memorize the following sentence which contains six ways:

A **rough**-coated, **dough**-faced, but **thoughtful** man walked to **Slough coughing throughout.**

Think yourself lucky you're not English English or you would have to remember that he was a **ploughman** (plowman), that he was **thorough** (which doesn't rhyme with **dough** in English English) and that he **hiccoughed** (hiccupped), too!

8 Remember the Face 1

The brain is very good at facial recognition. It must juggle with and store an extraordinary amount of variable information to be able to recognize a face. If you do not believe this, try to draw a picture of someone you know well. We can also recognize people's faces at different time periods in their lives—even if we never knew them at a particular age. How many of these famous people can you name?

a)

b)

c)

d)

e)

f)

g)

h)

i)

j)

9 Remember the Face 2

We have stored in our heads an extensive rogue's gallery of likenesses.
Identify these well-known figures:

a)

b)

c)

d)

e)

f)

g)

h)

i)

j)

10 ✱ Remember the Face 3

Identify these fictional characters:

a)

b)

c)

d)

e)

f)

g)

h)

i)

j)

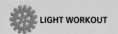 LIGHT WORKOUT    GETTING HARDER...   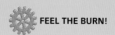 FEEL THE BURN!

11 Match the Grown-up

Can you figure out who these characters became when they grew up?

a)

b)

c)

d)

e)

f)

g)

h)

i)

j)

12a Memorize the Face

Look at these completely unknown characters and their names.
Then turn the page over.

Anita Mehta

Lucille Belmont

Daniel Olaye

Adrienne Aucoin

Emma Jane Sandelson

Craig Neilssen

Jennifer Mendez

Margaret Hanson

Michael Johnson

Angus Williams

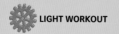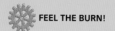
12b 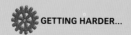 Memorize the Face

How many of these characters can you identify?

a)

b)

c)

d)

e)

f)

g)

h)

i)

j)

13 Mnemonics 1

One elementary technique for remembering a list of things is to invent a mnemonic using the first letter of each item. It is particularly useful for remembering lists of things when the order is important. So, for example, a way to recall the order of the cardinal points of the compass as you move clockwise might be: Never Eat Shredded Wheat (North, East, South, and West).

Can you identify what these mnemonics are for?

a) Big Elephants Can Always Understand Small Elephants.

b) Richard Of York Gave Battle In Vain.

c) My Very Excellent Mother Just Showed Us Nine Planets.

d) Eddie Ate Dynamite. Good-Bye, Eddie!

e) My Judy Really Makes Splendid Belching Noises.

14 Mnemonics 2

Things are easier to remember if you assimilate them into your own existing knowledge. Make up your own mnemonics for the things to be remembered in the previous question. And remember: The more bizarre or outrageous the mnemonic, the easier it is to remember.

15 Mnemonics 3

Devise your own ways of remembering the following information:

a) The fact that when you play chess and you are white, then the square that is farthest right on the board on your side must also be white.

b) The safe way to dilute an acid is by adding the acid to the water and not the other way around!

c) That in Fahrenheit (°F), water freezes at 32° and boils at 212° Fahrenheit.

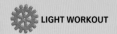 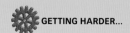
16 Objects

Look at this collection of objects for 5 minutes. Try to think of a way of remembering them. Then close the book and write a list of as many of the objects as you can remember.

17 Suits

Make up your own way of remembering the following:

a) Clubs, Diamonds, Hearts, and Spades (The order of the suits does not have any particular significance, so you are free to choose any order that makes for an easy mnemonic.)

b) The things you need to check before a long car journey: gasoline, battery, radiator water, tires, oil, and lights

c) The order of potting balls in the English game of snooker, which is: yellow, green, brown, blue, pink, black

18 South America

The names of the countries
of South America:

Argentina

Bolivia

Brazil

Chile

Colombia

Ecuador

French Guiana

Guyana

Paraguay

Peru

Suriname

Uruguay

Venezuela

How many names are on this
list? Devise a mnemonic for
the list and try to memorize it.
Is it easier to memorize such a
list when written in an aligned
vertical stack than when written
in a horizontal list as follows?

**Argentina, Bolivia,
Brazil, Chile, Colombia,
Ecuador, French Guiana,
Guyana, Paraguay, Peru,
Suriname, Uruguay,
Venezuela**

19 Zodiac

Devise a mnemonic for the 12
signs of the Zodiac shown below
in order and memorize it:

**Aries, Taurus, Gemini,
Cancer, Leo, Virgo, Libra,
Scorpio, Sagittarius,
Capricorn, Aquarius,
and Pisces**

20 Acronyms

The previous mnemonics were all
acronyms. That is to say, we chose
a sentence in which the words
began with the same letters as the
name we wanted to remember. But
trying to remember something is an
act of association, like hanging an
unfamiliar coat on a familiar hook.
A friend of mine taught his children
to distinguish between African and
Indian elephants by pointing out
that the ears of an African elephant
are shaped a little like Africa and
those of an Indian elephant resemble
the shape of India. When devising
a mnemonic be as playful and
imaginative as you can be.

8.

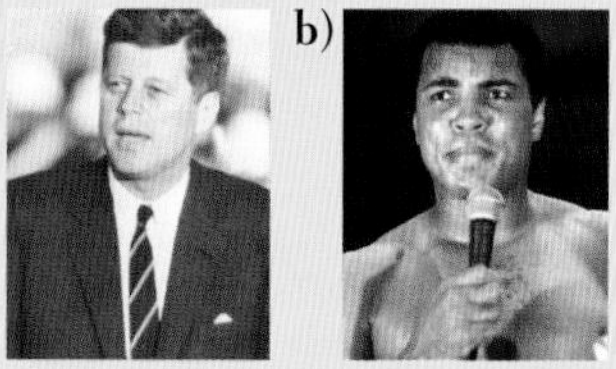

a)
President John
F. Kennedy

b)
Muhammed Ali

c)
Luciano Pavarotti

d)
Marylin Monroe

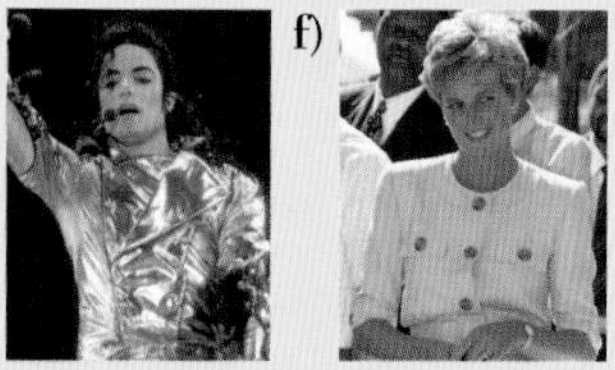

e)
Michael Jackson

f)
Princess Diana

g)
Martin Luther
King Jr.

h)
Pablo Picasso

i)
Pelé

j)
Bruce Lee

9.

a)
Shakespeare

b)
Albert Einstein

c)
Fred Astaire

d)
Elvis Presley

e)
George
Washington

f)
Abraham Lincoln

g)
Mother Teresa

h)
Mahatma Gandhi

i)
Winston
Churchill

j)
Henry VII

10.

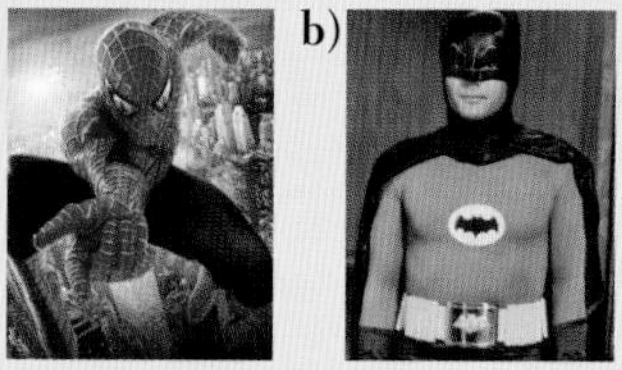

a)
Spider-Man

b)
Batman

c)
Mickey Mouse

d)
Dontatello
(Teenage Mutant
Ninja Turtle)

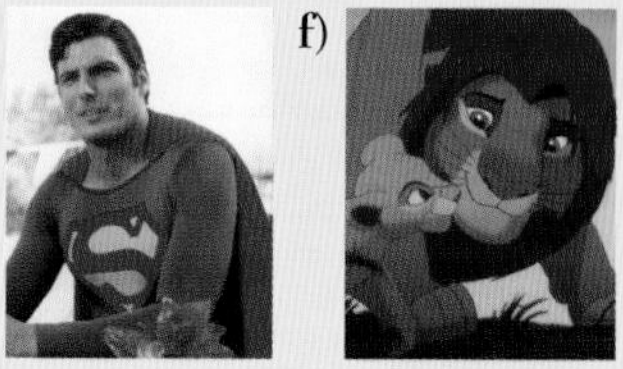

e)
Superman

f)
Simba and
Mufasa (Lion
King)

g)
Winnie the
Pooh

h)
Harry Potter

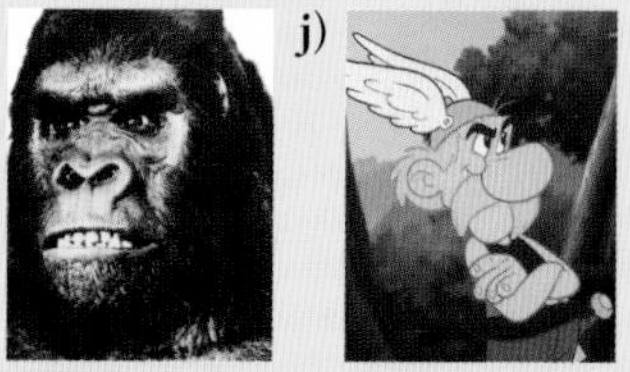

i)
King Kong

j)
Asterix
(French Cartoon)

11.

a)
Drew Barrymore

b)
Shirley Temple

c)
Jodie Foster

d)
Elijah Wood

e)
Elizabeth Taylor

f)
Macaulay Culkin

g)
Kylie Minogue and Jason Donovan

h)
Christian Bale

i)
James Dean

j)
Michael Jackson

12b.

a)
Michael Johnson

b)
Lucille Belmont

c)
Angus Williams

d)
Anita Mehta

e)
Margaret Hanson

f)
Adrienne Aucoin

g)
Jennifer Mendez

h)
Craig Neilssen

i)
Daniel Olaye

j)
Emma Jane Sandelson

13.

a) How to spell BECAUSE.

b) The colors of the rainbow in order: Red, Orange, Yellow, Green, Blue, Indigo, and Violet.

c) The order of the planets outward from the Sun: Mercury, Venus, Earth, Mars, Jupiter, Saturn, Uranus, Neptune, Pluto. Recently Pluto was demoted from being a planet, but it is still in the same place!

d) The notes of the strings on a guitar: EADGBE.

e) The names of champagne bottles in increasing size. The numbers in parentheses are the number of standard bottles contained in each one:

Magnum (2), Jeroboam (4), Rehoboam (6), Methusaleh (8), Salmanazar (12), Balthazar (16), and Nebuchadnezzar (20).

16.

Dinosaur

Cloud

Shoe

Car

Spoon

Frog

Comet

Tree

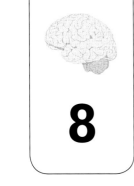

8

Get Creative

Now you've arrived at what may be the toughest part of your brain fitness program: sharpening your creativity.

Creativity is an area of mental activity that causes us as much delight as it does frustration. The pleasure of producing a work of art or cooking a delicious meal is one of the great satisfactions of being human. However, creativity is notorious for its habit of going on vacation just when you want it, or arriving in a flash of inspiration when you least expect it. While it may not be possible to turn you into Mozart or Einstein, by working the neural pathways in the right hemisphere of your brain, you will start to find lateral thinking easier.

Creativity is a vital quality of the human brain that, like memory, is essential for every activity. But it's difficult to describe and almost as hard to practice. So let's see what actually happens when the creative process works.

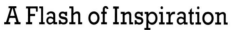

A Flash of Inspiration

Tackling a creative challenge is like no other brain puzzle. Usually there is nothing in the puzzle to guide you beyond the initial question. In a math puzzle, the information you're given is the clue to how to tackle finding the solution. The same applies to verbal and spatial puzzles.

With creative puzzles, though, there's usually no clear route from reading the question to working out the answer. Bridging that gap depends on being able to ignite your brain's creativity—what psychologists call the "Aha!" moment—when the answer (or at least the next step to finding it) jumps into your mind with a blinding flash of inspiration.

Though we don't always know how to kick-start this inspiration, we know what happens on a physical level. In 2004 Northwestern University researchers in the United States were monitoring brain activity among volunteers who had to solve lateral-thinking puzzles—puzzles in which the route linking question to answer was far from clear. They found that ⅓ of a second before the moment of inspiration that cleared the mental blockage, there was a surge of electrical activity within the right temporal lobe of the brain, a site that showed much less activity when solving more straightforward problems.

One explanation may be that this part of the brain specializes in amassing distantly related bits of information to make it easier to form the connections with the novel circuits in the left-hand part of the brain that are needed to solve creative problems.

Additional research turned up more information. Checking electro-encephalogram (EEG) readings, which monitor the brain's electrical activity, revealed that one and a half seconds before the "Aha!" moment, there was a smaller burst of lower-frequency activity in that same section of the brain, which led up to the "Aha!" moment itself. This may suggest that this first stage of temporal lobe activity is effectively gearing up the brain for its flash of inspiration by preparing the circuits needed for solution finding.

Give your brain some downtime

What can this tell us that will help in solving creative puzzles? The Northwestern researchers found in a later project that it was possible to "prepare the mind" to make the "Aha!" moment more likely to happen. So before we look at how to solve creative puzzles, let's take a moment to consider how best to achieve this condition. Rest, sleep, and freedom from tension all help keep brain performance at its highest level. Tuning out distractions through deep breathing and meditation helps, too.

Tune and focus

Focus is also needed. Consciously thinking in terms of a change of approach to problems is key. So the first section of puzzle questions included with this chapter doesn't ask for answers. It gives advice on how to perform this tuning-and-focusing process as effectively as possible, through peace and quiet and freedom from distractions or interruptions. It underlines the value of techniques for breathing, meditating, and emptying the mind of all unnecessary information to leave it fully open to the task ahead.

Think outside the box

Let's assume you've reached the point where you're focused and ready to tackle a specific creative puzzle. You don't want to sit there passively and hope inspiration will just turn up. So what can you do to jump-start your brain further?

Always remember that in creative puzzles and challenges, deciding how to solve the problem is usually much more difficult than finding the solution.

Creative puzzles can't be categorized the same way as mathematical, verbal, or spatial puzzles. But it's still worth trying as many as possible, and if you can't solve them easily, then learn from the answers. See where and how the inspirational jump had to be deployed to bridge the gap to the solution.

In an earlier chapter, for example, there was a series of numbers for which you had to find the next number in the series (see page 105). The mathematical way of solving the question is to work out the rules controlling the relationship of each number in the series to the one before it and the one after it—work that out, and you can easily predict the next number correctly.

That one question, however, defied that method completely. The numbers making up the series seemed completely random, but they weren't. The rule they followed was simple, but completely non-mathematical. The rule? Each successive number was the same as the number of letters in successive words of the question. Pick the next word, count the letters, and you had the answer.

Chances are you may never find another puzzle where that same trick would work. But being aware of the kind of twists and turns a puzzle strategy can take is likely to help you make that inspirational jump with a different problem.

Ramp It Up

In addition to preparing your brain for that specific moment in which it explodes into creative thought, you can actually keep it primed to do so. If you have the time, you can learn how to play a musical instrument or speak a foreign language. Here are a few suggestions for simpler and quicker ways to achieve the same effect.

Deciding how to solve the problem is usually more difficult than finding the solution.

Play with words

Other simpler and quicker ways to exercise creativity include devising new ways of describing people or places with humor, sharpness, affection, or anger. Try inventing new words, maybe combining existing words to describe a combination of two dissimilar things or people. Or draw up a list of complicated words and work out as many rhymes as you can for them. Then try building them into a limerick or a simpler four-line poem called a clerihew, where the first pair of lines rhyme and the second pair rhyme differently.

Debate

Join in a discussion of controversial subjects with many different facets. Every moment will stimulate your brain.

Create your own puzzle

Finally, why not try creating a puzzle of your own? Many people enjoy crosswords, but far fewer are able to create one. Yet devising the grid, choosing the solutions, and working out cryptic clues that are neither too difficult nor too easy exercises every cell in your brain—including the ones that give birth to creativity.

Tackling the Puzzles

The puzzles that follow will test your ability to find the inspiration that will lead to an apparently impossible solution. All you have to do is tackle the problem by a different route than you normally would—by literally approaching it from a different angle to the norm.

Take puzzle 25 on page 158 about the incorrectly labeled cans. If you find out what one of them actually contains, you can eliminate it from the reckoning. This then gives you a handle on working out what the correct labeling for the other two would be.

So what kind of simple outside test can distinguish the contents of one can from another? Shaking them might reveal which one contains the soup, from the noise of the liquid inside. Check the label on that and then work out the logic of the labels on the other two (given that they're all labeled incorrectly) to work out what each one contains.

The same applies to the other puzzle questions. If one asks you to put more letters or numbers into a grid than the spaces allow, then you have to ask how one space can contain more than one letter or number—maybe by turning one of them upside down or on its side. Try it and see. Keep your eyes open for visual puns or pictures drawn to conceal what they really contain.

So keep thinking, keep an open mind, and look for new kinds of creative challenges. And most important, don't be deterred if the answer seems impossible. As you work out more and more puzzles, your creativity will improve by leaps and bounds!

Creativity on Demand

Most of the difficulty we experience in using our creative power is getting it to work when we want it to. Australian researchers at the University of Sydney are working toward a thinking cap, a helmet carrying a complex series of connections that can calm or stimulate different sections of the brain when needed.

After studying the brain patterns of savants—people who show extraordinary levels of brain performance in doing certain specific tasks—the researchers have succeeded in identifying how savant brains are able to cope with damage in some areas by overcompensating in others. The helmet creates a similar effect by using tiny magnetic pulses to calm overactive areas and trigger underactive sections into working harder. The result is a measurable boost in artistic, creative, mathematical, and spatial-awareness skills.

Researchers hope eventually to produce a commercial device that will allow users to boost brain performance in selected areas whenever needed.

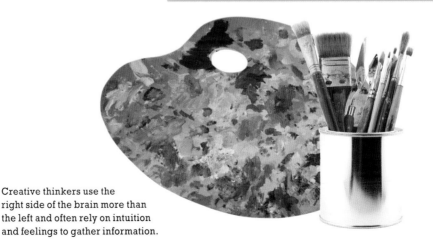

Creative thinkers use the right side of the brain more than the left and often rely on intuition and feelings to gather information.

Empty Your Mind

To boost your memory, creativity, or problem-solving abilities, it is worth improving focus and concentration and cultivating mental calm. However, it is hard to be mentally calm if you are not physically at peace.

Identify a space

The first task is to identify a space, a quiet corner, where you can remain undisturbed. This means being away from ringing telephones and cell phones, the sounds of radio, television, and—above all—a place where no one will interrupt you or speak to you. If your environment is not a completely peaceful one, you need to change it so that it is. Here are a few suggestions for private time: relaxing in the tub, floating in a private pool, sitting in a church or synagogue when there is no service, or going for a long country walk.

Take time out

Make a habit of taking time out and emptying your mind of all thoughts. Think about your daily schedule and choose a time when you can be sure of being undisturbed; make this a regular appointment with yourself. Turn off all radios, televisions, and phones.

Breathe

A useful way of clearing out repetitive and stressful thoughts is to concentrate on

Find a space where can be alone and empty your mind.

your breathing. Sit up or lie down, breathe in deeply, and hold your breath for a few seconds. It is useful to place your hands on the sides of your rib cage so that you can feel your ribs extending and contracting.

Then breathe out as slowly and completely as you can. Repeat this process until your breathing is regular and calm. Now start the relaxation process. Begin by wiggling your toes. Then relax them. Travel up the body, tensing each set of muscles in turn and then letting go so that they relax. Continue until you reach the top of your head. Repeat this whole process. Learn to recognize this state of calm and become more aware of it.

Do nothing

Practice doing nothing. If you are fidgety, sit still. If you are a talker, be quiet. Listen to and become aware of any residual sounds around you. Become aware of your surroundings and concentrate on them. Exclude thoughts of elsewhere. Be where you are. Then allow your thoughts to freewheel. Arrange to have daydreaming time every day, if possible, at a reproducible time. The value of this is that it returns the mind to its grounded state. The mind needs both action and inaction to work at its best.

Sometimes it is difficult to completely empty your mind, so it may help to focus on a single concept, such as breathing, or an object in the room. This will deter you from being distracted. To further cultivate this feeling of calm and concentration, you could join a yoga class.

Use time productively

Nevertheless, there are moments when emptying your mind isn't the most practical use of your time. For example, when waiting in the doctor's office or sitting in a traffic jam. It is better to use these moments to do something creative and useful. In a doctor's waiting room, it is useful to rehearse the questions you want to ask the doctor. There is nothing more frustrating than leaving the doctor's office and realizing that you still have more questions.

Frustrating long commutes or time spent in traffic jams can be turned into positive experiences. For example, you can learn a foreign language, or listen to music or books on CDs.

"All that we are is the result of what we have thought. The mind is everything. What we think, we become."

—BUDDHA

Creative Puzzles

Trying to pull creativity out of an untrained brain can be frustrating. Unless you have natural creative ability, there are some easy exercises and puzzles you can do to boost your imagination and your ability to "think outside the box." Try something from this section every day and you'll soon notice the difference.

1 Sequence

This puzzle is only for the discerning!

Which of the boxes below comes next?

a)   b)   c)   d)   e)

2 Full House

Write one digit per cell so that all the digits from 0 through 9 appear one way or another. Leave one of the cells empty:

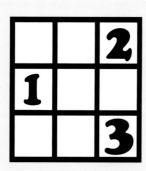

3 Word Games

What word is written here?

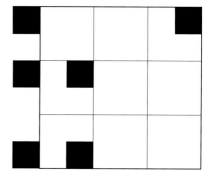

4 ❋ Letters

Write one letter per cell so that all 26 letters of the alphabet may be found there one way or another.

A	B	C	D	E	F
G					

6 ❋ Objects

Think of an object and then try to represent it using the tangram pieces. Not all objects you think of will be easy to represent! Here are a few to get you started:

a) A swan
b) A bird in flight
c) A bat
d) A house
e) A boat

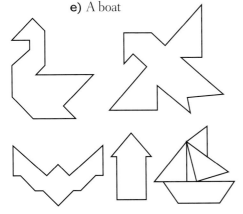

5 ❋ Tangram

Get hold of a tangram set. If you can't find one, you can always make one by taking a square piece of cardboard and dividing it into the seven shapes shown in this diagram.

You could consider getting a magnetic one, the pieces of which can be slid around on the refrigerator and freezer doors. Arrange the pieces to make a shape that you find aesthetically pleasing. The less obvious the shape, the better. Now invent a description of what it might represent. Here are a few examples of shapes you could describe:

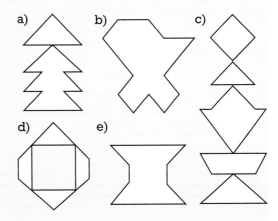

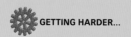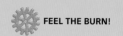
7 Outlines

If you have a partner or someone to compete with, decide together some things to represent and a time limit. Learning proceeds less tiresomely in a game, and the social interaction adds another dimension to the process. To increase the fun, you can try it against the clock. Here are some more outlines for you to try.

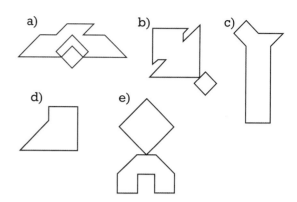

8 Uses

Think up as many bizarre uses as you can for familiar objects. The more bizarre your ideas, the better.

a) A coat hanger
b) A rubber band
c) A button
d) A broom
e) A CD

9 Sequence

Here is a sequence of numbers:

1   2   3

It is easy to say why the next number in the sequence could be 4. Make up a reason for why it could be 5. Can you think of other ways to continue the sequence?

10 Paper Clips

How many different uses can you think of for a paper clip?

11 Missing

The missing digit could be 1. But if it isn't, what could it be?

1111111111111111111111*111

12 Absurd Pairings

What do a tomato and a computer have in common? What is the difference between a raven and a writing desk? Think up absurd pairings of your own that on the face of it are unlinked, such as a cloud and a teaspoon. Then try to forge a link!

13 Write

Write the number 18 without taking your pen off the paper.

14 Odd Man Out

A cat, a sailor, and a table. Make up reasons why each one in turn might be the odd man out.

16 Aliens

Pretend you are an alien from the planet Zarg. People there do not age and do not speak. Send a postcard home about Earth dwellers.

18 Poetry

Try your hand at writing short poems. A poem is an attempt to crystallize ideas, insights, and feelings. The idea is to encapsulate a complex situation in a few well-chosen words.

20 Design a Country

Design a fictional country. Paint in the rivers and the towns and something of the environment. Name the cities. Make it sound as exotic as possible: the sort of country that would make you want to visit!

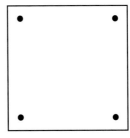

15 Social Interaction

Join a writing club, debating team, or discussion group. Learning can be enhanced in social interaction.

17 More Than One Way

The shape below can be divided into three pieces that reassemble to make a square as shown. Now find another way.

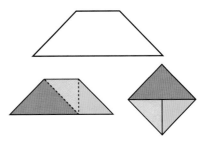

19 Origami

Take up origami. We spend most of our time living in a three-dimensional world, so we are naturally poor at thinking in terms of what happens when we fold the simplest shapes. Fold the piece of paper below so that the dots all lie in a straight line.

21 ✦ Board Games

Invent a new board game. Give yourself a setting such as a race track or a business. Design four game pieces and a board to travel around, and invent a set of rules. Don't just invent, try it out. See if you can tweak the rules to make the game more exciting and varied and, above all, to even out the players' chances.

23 ✦ Trick Questions

Make up your own trick questions. Try them out on others and get feedback. Here are a few to give you the general idea.

a) What lies between heaven and Earth?

b) What was Richard III's middle name?

c) What can you hold in your left hand but not in your right hand?

d) Tom's ma had 5 children. The first was called Baba, the second Bebe; the third Bibi; the fourth Bobo. What was the fifth called?

e) You have three melons in one hand and two in the other hand. What do you have?

22 ✦ Pictures

Take up sketching, painting, or cartooning. This will encourage you to look at the world in your own way. When you write a shopping list, draw pictures rather than writing the words.

24 ✦ Limericks

When driving, make up limericks using the names of the places you pass. They don't have to be good, but they do have to scan!

There was a young cyclist from Hull
Who was chased round a field by a bull.
He said, "Say what you like,"
As he pedaled his bike,
"But life in the country ain't dull!"

25 ✦ Cans

You have three cans. One contains peanuts. Another contains soup. And the final one contains cashew nuts. But each of the three cans has been mislabeled with the label of one of the others. How can you most simply work out what each can contains?

26 ❋ Lateral Puzzles

Lateral puzzles are usually presented as having a single answer. See if you can figure out the expected answers in the cases listed below. Then think up alternative solutions. They don't have to be plausible—they just need to be explicable!

a) There is a spot of my blood on the ceiling. How did it get there?

b) A man's life is saved because his car ran out of gas. How come?

c) Everyone had come in through the doors. The doors were not locked, but nobody could get back out. Why?

d) You run backward but move forward. How is this possible?

e) Which timepiece has the fewest moving parts? Which has the most moving parts?

27 ❋ Find Your Way Out

Can you discover a way out of the following predicaments?

a) Place a pencil where you can't step over it. Where could that be?

b) You are in a big room with a flat floor. A huge ball is rolling toward you. It is twice as high as you are tall. The doors and windows are locked. Where do you hide?

c) A Ping-Pong ball has fallen down a vertical pipe whose top is flush with the ground. It is too narrow to get your hand down. How can you retrieve the ball?

d) Two boys who were fighting are told to stand on a sheet of the same newspaper, but they cannot touch each other. How is this possible?

e) There are two long ropes each hanging from a strong ring fixed in the ceiling next to each other. You have a knife and can climb up one of the ropes without any difficulty. How can you end up with as much rope as possible?

 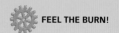
28 Think Actively

Make use of breaks in the day to think actively. In modern life, there are always boring moments. Traffic jams, waiting for a bus, a subway ride. Rather than fuming, you can use these fragments of time creatively. There is a difference between active and passive activities. Solving a crossword puzzle or observing what is happening around you is active. Reading a book is passive.

29 Learning Opportunities

When driving an automobile, you can't solve crosswords or other puzzles. But you can listen to the radio, a CD, or an MP3 player. However, there are even better ways to use this time. If you listen to language CDs, you can pick up a new language. Being able to say even a few words in a different language livens up the language centers in the brain.

30 Creative Exercise

As you drive along, there are many things you can do to exercise your creative faculties. A game that can be fun on long journeys is to take the three letters on a license plate and pretend they are an acronym for something. For example:

PSD   Purple Sprout Deniers

NAJ   National Association of Jailbirds

VOP   Very Old Person

ULA   Unusually Large Aardvark

CXW   Canadian X-ray Watchers

31 Alphabet Soup

A manufacturer of alphabet soup included only the letters A, C, I, L, M, N, R, U, V, W, Z, and one other. Which one? Why?

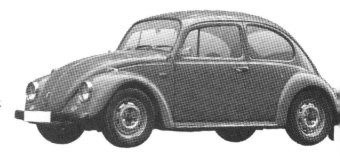

32 Puzzling

Take up puzzles and games. Puzzles encourage you to explore and think. Word searches are good exercises for detailed perception. Jigsaws are great for hand-eye coordination. Sudoku improves concentration and logic skills. Brainteasers help you to evolve your own strategies in thinking: You have to invent a way to crack the nut! Cryptic crosswords enable you to take words apart and view them differently. Take up chess or checkers.

Creativity is building a bridge between the present (the means) and the future. So planning ahead is a useful skill. In a game like chess, the possibilities are narrowed according to which moves you make. It is also a social interaction and is therefore easier to motivate. Trying to anticipate the moves the other person will make is a good creative exercise.

33 Logo

A friend of mine saw a truck bearing the name Abacus. Its logo was—of course—a picture of an abacus. He suggested that the company's advertising slogan could be: "You can count on us." Make up fake companies, then think up a logo and a witty advertising slogan.

34 Punning Dishes

Make up punning dishes. For example, here are a few on the menu of a restaurant that offers entrées named after celebrities:

Jack Lemmon Sole

Paella Fitzgerald

Leonard Cohen Chowder

Condoleeza Rice Pudding

Can you think of more?

 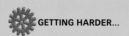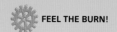
35 Wordplay

In cryptic crosswords the definitions rely on a play on words. See if you can solve these clues:

a) I may have it (3)

b) GEGS (9, 4)

c) HIJKLMNO (5)

d) Written in stone (10)

e) Part exchange? (5, 10)

Now make up your own cryptic clues. Try them out on others! Don't forget to ask for feedback.

37 Punning Books

Make up a list of silly book titles and authors that play off each other and make a pun. The sillier, the better. Here are some examples:

Carpeting by Walter Wall

Cliff Accident by Eileen Dover

Where's My Hat? by Sonia Head

Big Game by Hugh Jelliphant

Wines I Have Known by M. T. Bottle

36 Charades

In charades you have to represent a book or movie title by acting out ideas, without using words, to suggest the title. You don't have to give every word—just the important words that will enable the people guessing to figure out what they represent.

38 Classic Match

Here is a classic matchstick puzzle that uses five squares. Move as few matches as possible to leave four squares. You may not remove the matches. Make up your own matchstick puzzles. Try your puzzle out on a friend. Feedback is an important part of the creative process!

39 ⚙ Shapes

Divide the shape below into three pieces that can be reassembled to make a rectangle. Here is one way. How many other ways can you find?

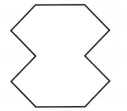

Be Inspired

De-clutter your living and working spaces to clear your mind. A tidy and organized environment allows creative juices to flow. Or seek out natural beauty. Whether it's getting up in time to watch the sunrise, or taking a walk through the park in fall, nature fuels creative inspiration.

NEUROBIC TIP

40 ⚙ Riddles

Below are a number of riddles that have stumped people over the years. How many can you answer?

a) What runs but never walks?

b) What's black and white and red all over?

c) What we caught, we threw away; what we didn't catch, we kept.

d) What do you sit on, sleep on, and brush your teeth with?

e) He who makes it doesn't tell. He who takes it doesn't know it. He who knows it doesn't want it. What is it?

Make up a few of your own.

1. In each shape you can see the final letters of the alphabet in order. So the answer is *e*, in which we may discern a Z.

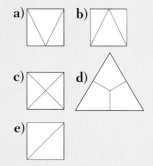

a)   b)

c)   d)

e)

2. The heavy style of the digits already written are perhaps a clue. Nine is omitted, as 6 will give us a 9 when viewed the other way around. The central square is left empty so that the whole array becomes a sort of zero.

3. LIFE. Hold the page horizontal and look at it from a low angle. It is, of course, written upside down! In life it often pays to look at things from different points of view.

4. Since *N* becomes *Z* if seen on its side and *M* becomes *W*, we include only one of *N* or *Z* and one of *W* or *M*. The omitted letters are apparent if we view the grid from another angle.

A	B	C	D	E	F
G	H	I	J	K	L
M	N	O	P	Q	R
S	T	U	V	X	Y

5.

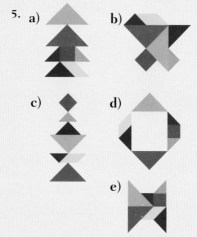

a)   b)

c)   d)

e)

6.

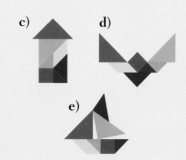

a)   b)

c)   d)

e)

7.

a)

b)   c)

d)   e)

9. These are whole numbers whose names end in a vowel.

11. Here is one possible solution: The numbers represent the numbers of syllables in the names of the letters of the alphabet. These all contain one syllable except for *W*, which contains three. So the asterisk could be replaced by 3. This question shows that the obvious answer isn't always the only possiblity.

13. One way is to draw the number in a frame. You need to start at one of the two points marked with a cross.

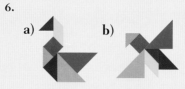

Alternatively you can fold the corner of the paper over, draw the 1, and continue onto the back of the paper, slipping back onto the side you are writing the number on, thereby completing the 8.

Both of these two methods involve writing more than the 18 demanded. One makes a virtue of this extra by adding a frame; the other hides it away on the back of the paper.

17.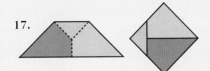

19. Fold the square into quarters. Then fold back the two outside quarters:

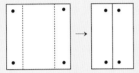

Then fold back as shown.

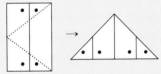

23. a) The word "and"
b) "The"
c) Your right elbow
d) Tom
e) Big hands

25. If the nuts rattle, you have it made, since soup doesn't. You know the one labeled "soup" contains nuts, so ignore that. Instead you need to discover which of the cans labeled "cashew nuts" or "peanuts" contains the soup. Shake the can marked "cashew nuts." If it rattles, it contains peanuts. It then follows that the one marked "soup" contains cashews and the one marked "peanuts" contains soup.

If, instead, the can marked "cashew nuts" doesn't rattle, it contains the soup. Then it follows that the can labeled "peanuts" contains cashews and the one labeled "soup" contains peanuts.

Suppose that the nuts are packed so tightly that they do not rattle, then it is still in fact possible to tell by rolling the cans.

A can packed solidly will roll more easily than one in which there is a liquid. When you try to roll a can containing a liquid like soup the motion gets counteracted and slowed down very quickly by the movement of the liquid. So even if the nuts don't rattle, you can still work out what is what

26. Here are possible answers:
a) I squashed a mosquito which had bitten me.

b) He tried to commit suicide with a tube from the exhaust, but the engine cut out.

c) The doors opened inward, but the crowd pressed so hard in their attempts to get out that the doors could not be opened inward.

d) You are standing on a ball in the circus or on a log.

e) The sun dial has no moving parts; an hourglass has thousands of grains of sand in it.

Now think of answers on your own.

27. a) For example, next to the baseboard where the floor meets the wall.

b) Crouch down in the corner.

c) Pour water down the tube so that the ball floats to the top.

d) The newspaper is passed under the door and they stand on it in different rooms.

e) First knot the bottom ends of the ropes together. Then climb one rope and cut the other where it joins the ring

Then feed the free end through the ring you are suspended from until the knot joining the two ropes is at the ring. Then, holding both ropes, cut the knot attaching it to the ring. You now have one long rope passing through the ring. Holding both parts of the composite rope, slide down. Then pull the rope by one end so it slips free of the ring.

31. S. These are the letters with the two free ends.

35. a) Dot
b) Scrambled eggs
c) Water (H_2O = H to O!)
d) Heiroglyph
e) Organ transplant

38. We need move only two matches, as shown.

39.

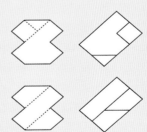

40. a) A river
b) A sunburned zebra; a newspaper
c) Fleas
d) A chair, a bed and a toothbrush
e) A coffin

9

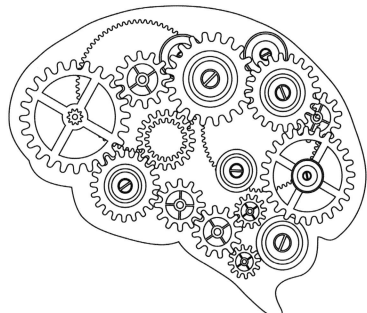

Brain Conditioning

No brain-training regime can work unless it is accompanied by a healthy diet and regular physical exercise. An unbalanced diet, irregular eating, low fluid intake, smoking and drinking heavily, and other lifestyle choices all affect the brain's fitness and stamina. A well-nourished, physically fit body is just as important to your brain's ability to think and remember as mental exercises that maximize its potential. That's because your brain is literally made from substances in the food you eat, while exercise actually triggers the growth of new brain cells. Here's how to use food and exercise to—literally—build a better brain.

Feed Your Brain

Think you'll skip breakfast? That kind of thinking only proves you need to eat! Your brain cells and the neurotransmitters that flash messages between those little power centers are made from the carbs, proteins, and fats in the food you eat.

Carbs in your morning toast provide the raw materials to make a neurotransmitter called serotonin, which directly influences how well you learn something new and whether you remember it.

Protein in your egg provides the raw material to make three other neurotransmitters that influence how well you can focus and pay attention to what it is you're trying to learn and remember—and how well you think.

What's more, the fats found in milk help those neurotransmitters move around and do their jobs. One dietary fat in particular—the omega-3 fatty acid found in fish such as salmon—is suspected to directly impact how well you remember.

Maybe you should try some smoked salmon with your egg this morning? Here are some other suggestions.

Pile on protein

Ideally, protein needs to provide between 10 to 20 percent of the body's total calorie intake each day, bearing in mind that each gram of protein contains 4 calories. Individual helpings need to be around 8 ounces (230 g) a day for men and 5 ounces (140 g) for women, from the leanest sources available. These include fish—especially oily fish such as salmon, fresh (not canned) tuna, and mackerel—and other seafood, ideally eaten twice a week.

For the greatest benefit, food needs to be broiled, roasted, or microwaved rather than fried, with the excess fat drained away afterward. Other good sources of protein include chicken, eggs, low-fat milk and cheese, and soy protein foods for vegetarians, such as tofu, soymilk, and textured vegetable protein as a meat substitute.

Find the right carbs

Carbohydrates, which provide mental and physical energy, amount to 35 percent of the ideal daily calorie intake.

Heavier carbohydrates, such as bread, potatoes, rice, and pasta, contain a higher proportion of starch, which some experts say tends to impair the clarity of brain function before undertaking especially challenging mental tasks. Yet since it takes time to digest carbs fully, they can help maintain blood sugar and brain energy levels over a longer period.

Generally, unrefined carbohydrates such as brown or whole-wheat bread, rice, and pasta are better for you than the refined versions, because vital nutrients are stripped out when the bran and wheat germ are removed during the refining process.

Most nutrition scientists suggest you eat at least five servings of carb-rich fruits and vegetables every day. In fact, twice this amount is perfectly acceptable, especially in foods such as celery that are high in fiber but low in calories. Fresh fruits and vegetables can be supplemented by frozen, canned, or dried equivalents. And cruciferous (cabbage family) and leafy vegetables, such as cauliflower, lettuce, broccoli, or spinach, are known to improve performance in learning and memory tests.

In the United States, one Harvard University research program that studied the eating patterns of more than 13,000 nurses over a decade found that the higher the proportion of these vegetables that were included in the diet, the better the nurses' test performance.

Pick your fat

Fats, which experts suggest should account for 10 to 15 percent of your daily caloric intake, are also essential for a balanced diet because they help build cells and promote healthy cell function. What's more, some vitamins are absorbed by the body only if dissolved in fat. There are four kinds: saturated, trans, monounsaturated, and polyunsaturated.

Saturated fat is found in meat and dairy products and also in fat that's used for margarine or vegetable shortening (hydrogen atoms are added to keep these products solid at room temperature). Too much saturated fat can cause heart problems and narrowing of the arteries, which damages brain function.

Trans fat, which scientists now say is the worst fat you can eat, is partially saturated by adding hydrogen to improve shelf life and the taste and texture of food.

Focus on Breakfast

The best way to maintain brain energy levels is to eat at regular intervals, choosing foods that are slow to digest.

Breakfast is vital for concentration and mental productivity. Choosing a healthy breakfast means choosing whole-grain breads and cereals, fruits, skim or low-fat milk, and fruit juice. A study conducted at the University of Wales suggests that such a breakfast will boost concentration and memory. Other ingredients for promoting concentration and mental agility include yogurt, hard-boiled eggs, and low-fat muffins.

Mono-unsaturated fats lack two hydrogen atoms in each molecule, which makes them a healthy alternative. Studies show that a diet rich in monounsaturated fats reduces heart disease and stroke.

Polyunsaturates, which are found in whole-grain products, fish, and seafood, also play a role in lowering the risk of strokes and heart attacks.

Whichever fat you choose, keep in mind that a gram of fat contains nine calories—more than double the calories of proteins or carbohydrates.

Drink

Because water accounts for more than 50 percent of body weight, losses through perspiration and urination need to be replaced to avoid dehydration, which causes headaches and fatigue as well as impairing concentration and brain efficiency.

> "Lack of activity destroys the good condition of every human being ... movement and methodical physical exercise save it and preserve it."
>
> —PLATO

This means at least six to eight glasses of fluid each day, more during hot, dry weather. Fluids can be water, fruit juice, milk, tea, and coffee, but too much caffeine can increase anxiety, restlessness, and irritation. Too much alcohol can also cause health problems, though some studies have shown that a little alcohol, particularly in the form of red wine, may be beneficial.

Move It, Use It, Work It!

When you are simply lying around, regular signals pass to and from your brain about the positions of your limbs. But when walking, running, bicycling, or swimming, these messages are vastly multiplied, and the electrical activity they create builds up within the brain and causes the release of growth factors—naturally occurring chemicals that stimulate the creation of new neurons, the formation of new connections, and an increasingly complex and capable mental network.

Several studies support this idea. In an American study conducted by the University of Illinois, for example, a boost of between 5 and 7 percent in overall fitness was related to a boost of 15 percent in mental function. And in another study, male soccer players were given tactical game problems to solve before and after strenuous treadmill sessions, and female runners were given addition and subtraction exercises before and after training runs.

In both cases, mental performance improved after repeat exercises. Those activities release hormones essential for the brain's information-processing functions. According to experts, the effects may last up to an hour and a half after each exercise session.

Even low-level exercise can help. Because walking boosts circulation of blood and oxygen to the brain, the brain's own blood vessels are stimulated into growing. A test of senior walkers revealed that their memory, learning ability, concentration, and reasoning were improved over people of similar age who did not participate in regular exercise. Moreover, the more time spent walking, the greater the improvement. Additional tests showed that regular physical exercise boosted concentration, reaction speed, planning, organization, and multitasking.

In the United States, the Bronx Aging Study followed almost 500 people for more than 20 years. The results showed that people who took part in mentally stimulating physical games and other leisure activities several times a week had a 65–75 percent better probability of remaining sharp than those who did not.

Pick the best

There are three main levels of exercise—light, moderate, or vigorous, depending on the exertion involved.

Light exercise covers walking, gardening, or light housework, for example. Walking improves the condition of the heart and lungs and boosts bone

Sleep Recharges Your Brain

Slow-wave sleep—deep sleep not interrupted by dreams—plays a major role in improving the brain's ability to solve problems, according to research at the University of Lübeck in Germany. At the end of an evening, a group of 106 volunteers was shown a number puzzle containing a hidden code which had to be cracked to solve the problem. Half the volunteers were kept awake through the night, working on other problems, while the other half were free to enjoy a sound night's sleep. When they tackled the test again in the morning, twice as many of those who had slept well made the jump of inspiration needed to solve the problem, compared with those who had spent the night working. Even shorter naps improved brain function—research at the State University of New York showed these boosted memory by 15 percent.

density. It also trains the muscles of the lower body, but without the impact of running, which stresses the joints.

Moderate exercise usually makes you perspire and feel slightly out of breath because it makes more demands on the body. Walking becomes moderate exercise when performed briskly, or when walking uphill on a reasonably steep gradient.

Vigorous exercise causes rapid breathing and profuse sweating. Jogging, bicycling uphill or into the wind, and walking while carrying heavy bags or climbing steep slopes or long flights of steps all qualify as vigorous exercise.

In general, the more strenuous the exercise, the greater the benefit, but most studies confirm that even regular moderate exercise, such as a half-hour walk three times a week, has a beneficial effect on brain activity and efficiency.

One reason for this may be linked to the mechanism that allows the brain to control muscular activity through nerve action. Professor Jeff Lichtman of Washington University School of Medicine in St. Louis, Missouri, has found that a lack of physical activity produces a loss of nerve signals that damages the delicate mechanism for muscle control. Regular exercise that keeps the muscles active maintains the brain/muscle connections in peak condition.

But keep this in mind: Studies also show that too much exercise—working out until you're exhausted, for example— reverses any gains in brainpower you may have made.

Build your own exercise program

Regular exercise not only improves brain function, it also improves life expectancy and quality of life and reduces weight and the risk of heart disease, diabetes, and other serious conditions.

But making a regular exercise regime work effectively requires motivation. Recognizing the objectives of an exercise program, from improving brain function to losing excess weight, is vital to keep it going.

Choosing the right kind of exercise, exercising at your own pace, varying your routine to prevent boredom, and setting realistic rather than impossible goals, which causes frustration and disappointment, are all vital factors.

Here are three ways to make exercising a success.

Give your body a heads-up

A physical fitness routine that will promote a healthy brain begins before getting up in the morning. Simply moving

How to Get Started

Many experts advise a regime of at least 30 minutes of vigorous exercise a day to maintain fitness levels, including brain fitness. Others say that exercising three days a week is perfectly adequate.

Either way, reaching this level of fitness involves building up to it gradually, especially if starting from little or no regular exercise. If you decide to run regularly, for example, begin by walking. Then, after a week or so, add in a few short bursts of jogging interspersed with brisk walking, before progressively building up the pace and duration of each run.

Two caveats: One, if you haven't exercised in a while, check with your doctor first. Two, exercising to the point of exhaustion decidedly lessens brainpower. It wears down the body and trashes your immune system.

your toes more vigorously when you are waking helps to activate the nerves that radiate signals to the rest of your body, promoting energy and improving balance when you finally get out of bed. The exercise can be repeated whenever you've been sitting for prolonged periods.

Beat temptation

For the rest of the exercise program, most experts recommend at least 30 minutes of activity each day. The best way to find time for this and avoid the temptation to skip an exercise because of a crowded schedule is to fit exercise into the normal daily routine. If you drive to work and the distance is not too great, consider walking or bicycling instead. If you travel to and from work by bus or train, then consider getting off one or two stops early and walking the rest of the way. If distances are too great, then bicycle for the first stage of the outbound trip and the last leg of the trip home, and find somewhere secure to leave your bike at the train or bus station.

Brain Exercise? Walking!

Even people who have spent most of their adult lives avoiding exercise can benefit from its effects to a surprising extent.

Professor Arthur Kramer and his team at the University of Illinois recruited 214 volunteers between 60 and 75 years of age who hadn't been involved in regular exercise for at least 5 to 10 years, and in some cases for as much as 30 or 40 years.

After measuring how fit they were to begin with, they were split into two groups—half took long walks three times a week for six months, while the others did weight-training in the gym.

At the end of the program, the walkers were more fit both physically and mentally; they improved by around 5–7 percent in heart and lung function and were better at solving mental tests by up to 15 percent. The weight trainers were also fitter but did not show the same improvement in brain function.

Change your routine

A positive routine can help during leisure time, too. Walking a dog, either your own or someone else's, adds interest to what would otherwise be merely another exercise session. Stopping off for a swim on the way home from work improves both fitness and relaxation at the end of an otherwise stressful day. While traveling to work or at work, try to take the stairs rather than an elevator or an escalator. And always remember that getting up half an hour earlier and exercising before work carries maximum benefits of alertness and energy for the rest of the day.

Photo Credits

All other images are the copyright of Quintet Publishing Ltd. While every effort has been made to credit contributors, Quintet Publishing would like to apologize if there have been any omissions or errors—and would be pleased to make the appropriate corrections for future editions of the book.

T = top, *L* = left, *C* = center, *B* = bottom, *R* = right

p.2: Shutterstock; p.3: iStock; p.5: iStock; p.6: iStock; p.7: Shutterstock; p.9: Shutterstock; p.12: iStock; p.13 *L*: iStock, *R*: Shutterstock; p.14: iStock; p.17: Shutterstock; p.18; Shutterstock; p.20: iStock; p.21 *L*: iStock, *R*: Shutterstock; p.22: iStock; p.23: Shutterstock; p.24: Shutterstock; p.25: iStock; p.26: iStock; p.27 *L*: iStock, *R*: Shutterstock; p.28: Shutterstock; p.29: iStock; p.30: iStock; p.32: Shutterstock; p.34: p.37 *T*: © D. Hurst/Alamy, *BL*: BLOOMimage/Getty, *LC*: Shutterstock, *BCL*: © Ned Frisk Photography/Corbis, *CL*: Andy Crawford/Getty, *BCR*: Alex Cao/Getty, *CR*: Chris Stevens/Getty, *BR*: Jan Stromme/Getty. *RC*: Andy Crawford/Getty; p.41: Shutterstock; p.46 Shutterstock; p.48 *B*: Shutterstock, *C*: Shutterstock; p.49: Shutterstock; p.56: istock; p.58: Shutterstock; p.59: istock; p.60: istock; p.61: istock; p.78: Shutterstock; p.80 *T*: Shutterstock, *B*: istock; p.82: Shutterstock; p.86: Shutterstock; p.87: Shutterstock; p.92: Shutterstock; p.95: Shutterstock; p.98: istock; p.100: istock; p.101: istock; p.102: istock; p.124: istock; p.126: Shutterstock; p.131: Shutterstock; p.135 *FT*: © Trinity Mirror/Mirrorpix/Alamy, *TL*: © by Leo Mason/Alamy, *TC*: © Pictorial Press Ltd/Alamy, *TR*: © Mary Evans Picture Library/Alamy, *CL*: © MARKA/Alamy, *CC*: © Lionel Cherruault Royal Picture Library/Alamy, *CR*: © Mary Evans Picture Library/Alamy, *BL*: © Pictorial Press Ltd/Alamy, *BC*: © Alex Gotfryd/CORBIS, *BR*: © Pictorial Press Ltd/Alamy; p.136 *TL*: © Paul Springett A/Alamy, *TC*: © Pictorial Press Ltd/Alamy, *TR*: © Pictorial Press Ltd/Alamy, *CL*: © Pictorial Press Ltd/Alamy, *CC*: © Classic Image/Alamy, *CR*: © Classic Image/Alamy, *BL*: © Tim Graham/Alamy, *BC*: © Dinodia Images/Alamy, *BR*: © Pictorial Press Ltd/Alamy, *FBL*: © Lebrecht Music and Arts Photo Library/Alamy; p.137 *TL*: © United Archives GmbH/Alamy, *TC*: © Pictorial Press Ltd/Alamy, *TR*: © D. Hurst/Alamy, *CL*: © Paul Broadbent/Alamy, *CC*: © Pictorial Press Ltd/Alamy, *CR*: © Pictorial Press Ltd/Alamy, *BL*: © INTERFOTO/Alamy, *BC*: © Pictorial Press Ltd/Alamy, *BR*: © Pictorial Press Ltd/Alamy, *FBL*: © Photos 12/Alamy; p.138 *TL*: © Photos 12/Alamy, *TC*: © Photos 12/Alamy, *TR*: © Terry Fincher.Photo Int/Alamy, *CL*: © United Archives GmbH/Alamy, *CC*: © Pictorial Press Ltd/Alamy, *CR*: © Photos 12/Alamy, *BL*: © INTERFOTO/Alamy, *BC*: © Photos 12/Alamy, *BR*: © INTERFOTO/Alamy, *FBL*: © Pictorial Press Ltd/Alamy; p.139 *TL*: Shutterstock, *TC*: Shutterstock, *TR*: Shutterstock, *CL*: Shutterstock, *CC*: Shutterstock, *CR*: Shutterstock, *BL*: Shutterstock, *BC*: Shutterstock, *BR*: Shutterstock, *FBL*: Shutterstock; p.140 *TL*: Shutterstock, *TC*: Shutterstock, *TR*: Shutterstock, *CL*: Shutterstock, *CC*: Shutterstock, *CR*: Shutterstock, *BL*: Shutterstock, *BC*: Shutterstock, *BR*: Shutterstock, *FBL*: Shutterstock; p.141: Shutterstock; p.142: Shutterstock; p.143: Shutterstock; p.147: Shutterstock; p.148: Shutterstock; p.151: Shutterstock; p.157: Shutterstock; p.160: istock; p.161: istock; p.163: Shutterstock; p.167: istock; p.168: istock.